CASE STUDIES IN
EDUCATION AND CULTURE

———

General Editors

George *and* Louise Spindler
Stanford University

———

THEM CHILDREN
A Study in Language Learning

THEM CHILDREN

A Study in Language Learning

MARTHA COONFIELD WARD

HOLT, RINEHART AND WINSTON, INC.

New York   Chicago   San Francisco   Atlanta   Dallas
Montreal   Toronto   London   Sydney

Copyright © 1971 by Holt, Rinehart and Winston, Inc.
Library of Congress Catalog Card Number: 70-157882
ISBN: 0-03-086294-9
Printed in the United States of America
0 1 2 3   059   9 8 7 6 5 4 3 2 1

Foreword

About the Series

This series of case studies in education and culture is designed to bring to students in professional education and in the social sciences the results of direct observation and participation in educational process in a variety of cultural settings. Individual studies will include some devoted to single classrooms, others will focus on single schools, some on large communities and their schools; still others will report on indigenous cultural transmission where there are no schools at all in the western sense. Every attempt will be made to move beyond the formalistic treatments of educational process to the interaction between the people engaged in educative events, their thinking and feeling, and the content of the educational process in which they are engaged. Each study will be basically descriptive in character but since all of them are about education they are also problem-oriented. Interpretive generalizations are produced inductively. Some are stated explicitly by the authors of the studies. Others are generated in the reader's mind as hypotheses about education and its environmental relationships.

The cross-cultural emphasis of the series is particularly significant. Education is a cultural process. Each new member of a society or a group must learn to act appropriately as a member and contribute to its maintenance and, occasionally, to its improvement. Education, in every cultural setting, is an instrument for survival. It is also an instrument for adaptation and change. To understand education we must study it as it is—imbedded in the culture of which it is an integral part and which it serves.

When education is studied this way, the generalizations about the relationship between schools and communities, educational and social systems, education and cultural setting that are current in modern educational discussions, become meaningful. This series is, therefore, intended for use in courses in comparative and overseas education, social foundations and the sociology of education, international educational development, culture and personality, social psychology, cultural dynamics and cultural transmission, comparative sociology—wherever the interdependency of education and culture, and education and society, is particularly relevant.

We hope these studies will be useful as resources for comparative analyses, and for stimulating thinking and discussion about education that is not confined by one's own cultural experience. Without this exercise of a comparative, transcultural perspective it seems unlikely that we can acquire a clear view of our own educational experience, or view education in other cultural settings without ethnocentric bias.

About the Author

As a Junior High school teacher in Nashville, Tennessee, Martha Coonfield Ward became interested in the problems of children's language learning. Later in graduate school at Tulane University in New Orleans, she had the opportunity to investigate some of these ideas. She is currently Assistant Professor of Anthropology at Louisiana State University in New Orleans. For the year 1970–1971, she and her husband were anthropologists working in Ponape, Micronesia, on a medical research project sponsored by the University of North Carolina, Department of Epidemiology.

About the Book

This is a study of how children in a small community called Rosepoint in the vicinity of New Orleans acquire speech. The processes of language acquisition that Martha Ward describes in this community are of great significance to educators. The discongruities between the expectations of teachers and the child's background and experience, not only with respect to language behavior but also to other areas of social behavior, are at the base of many of the educational calamities occurring in the United States today. Though linguistic and social experience is different in each speech community, the experience of Rosepoint children is analogous to the experience of children in other places where the cultural context is not middle class.

The author provides essential contextualization for her problem. Family composition, life space, means used to control children, interaction between members of the household, are all dealt with. This all black community was formerly a plantation and many families counting as many as four living generations lived on the land when it was a producing plantation. Though some problems in relations between blacks and whites are not as acute at Rosepoint as elsewhere, the low pay, seasonal unemployment, and rampant paternalism in this sugarcane producing area duplicates the same conditions well documented for the cotton producing areas of the South. These problems are qualitatively somewhat different from those in the northern urban areas; however, quantitatively they may be no worse.

Dr. Ward made intensive observations as a participant-observer and interviewer in seven families. Her most productive research strategy was to take advantage of her almost complete access to her families to participate in the daily routine, taking notes and asking questions casually rather than formally. The author focuses on the child's linguistic contacts—to whom the child talks, who talks to him, what they talk about, when they need to talk—in an effort to define the range of linguistic opportunities.

In this community, where adults do not regard children as people to talk to, the author finds what might be called a "restricted code" as described by Bernstein.

An analysis is made of the way this code is acquired, including the use of extra-verbal channels, and through the interventions involved in social control. The situation appears unique to the middle class reader in that children who talk around adults are considered bad and wearing on the elders' nerves. The burden of the role of "teacher" of language falls to older children who often communicate misinformation. The author is careful to point out that the "restricted code" acquired is in no sense deficient in the environment in which the child acquires it. She points out that there is no "linguistically deprived" child in the strict sense of the word, and cites Lenneberg and others of his persuasion who assert that the basic processes and sequence of language learning are a part of a regular matura-tional process shared by all members of the human race irrespective of cultural differences. As the author says, "Any theory of language learning would have to explain Rosepoint, in which the children appear to receive little formal instruc-tion, and even less practice in their emerging skills." Rosepoint children not only learn to speak, but learn to speak appropriately and effectively in the Rosepoint environment.

The author poses a number of specific questions for educators, for example: of what relevance is test taking in a Rosepoint school where a child's total environ-ment is at variance with the culture of the school? Is the child who has only lived near the river and understands only "up the river, down the river, away from the river, and to the river" in place of north, south, east, and west, stupid? But the most important questions posed by this study are those relating most directly to language learning. The style of his learning, as well as the style of the speech learned, is very different in Rosepoint than in a middle-class home, white or black. What is the obligation of the school as this difference is faced? What-ever the answer, it seems clear that educators must understand language learning in Rosepoint, and many other places like it, if they are to function effectively with children from diverse cultural backgrounds.

Louise and George Spindler
General Editors

Preface

The major purposes of this research are to show specific examples of cultural transmission, to examine real-life conditions under which the children of the particular culture actually learn their language, and to explore the ways by which their families instill certain values through the use of language.

This book is dedicated to three people who taught me more than they realize: my husband, Roger; my teacher, Marshall; and my friend, Lydia. Lydia, her family and friends, fed me, answered my questions, and more than fulfilled their own standards of kindness. My advisor Marshall Durbin, now of Washington University in St. Louis, was a major inspiration in the planning, execution, and writing of this project. My husband, Roger, contributed many hours of patience and editing, as well as frequent trips with me to Rosepoint.

Other members of the Tulane University faculty and their spouses made special contributions. John L. Fischer, then chairman of the department, helped to secure financial support for the project, and made useful suggestions at every stage. Also invaluable was the encouragement of Professor Ann M. Fischer and Professor Munro Edmonson. Stephen Tyler, Mridula Adenwala Durbin, Barbara Edmonson, and Arden King read the manuscript and made many helpful suggestions. Mrs. Mable Glover, secretary of the Anthropology Department, will recognize her singular contribution, but may not realize the respect and appreciation she has earned. My sincere appreciation goes to George and Louise Spindler, and Dell Hymes, who helped in the preparation of the manuscript.

I wish I could thank personally all the people of Rosepoint. In the interests of preserving their privacy, I have changed all individual names as well as the name of their community. However, they will remember who among them befriended me. To those people, I extend my gratitude.

Martha Coonfield Ward

Contents

Foreword   v

Preface   ix

Introduction   1

1. The History and Ethnographic Background   5
   Rosepoint, 7
   The influence of transplanted French culture, 10
   Black-white relationships, 12

2. The Ethnographic Methodology   13
   The children's reactions as data, 14

3. The Family of Them Children   19
   Family "life-space" and composition, 19
   Characteristics of the household, 22
   Caretakers, 24
   Age-grading, 25
   Them children—values in child rearing, 27

4. A Rosepoint Child: The Boundary of Experience   31
   The daily routine, 32
   Weekly, monthly, and yearly routines, 35
   Non-kin encounters for children, 35
   Physical environment, 37
   Toys as part of the learning environment, 38
   Traveling: the "Charity Canal" complex, 40
   Other travels: "On the road," 41

5. "Teaching" Them Children to Talk   43
   Expansions, 43
   Characteristics of adults' speech to children, 47
   The contrast of adult to adult speech, 50
   Corrections and requests for information, 52
   Who are the teachers? 53
   Instructive functions, 54
   A theoretical problem, 56

6. Keeping Them Children Under Control   58
   Personal and positional families, 59
   Appeals, 60

Strategies and manipulation, 61
Threats, 63
Imperatives and appeals, 64
Disciplinary activities, 67
Verbal tricks in manipulation, 69
Children's manipulation of parents and other adults, 71
Interrogative functions, 72
The style of manipulation in Rosepoint, 74

7. "Playing Around": The Communication of Affection
   and Aggression   75
Affection and aggression, 75
Love games and linguistic routines, 77
Expressive communication, 79
Baby talk, 83
Affection exchanges, 84
Dancing, 85
The reparative function, 85
Expressive functions, 86

8. At Home and At School: Observations on Discontinuity   88
The school environment, 90
The conflict of home and school, 91
Dumb or deprived? 93
The values of the Rosepoint way, 93

Additional Readings   95
References Cited   97

Introduction

St. James Parish is fifty-five miles west of New Orleans on the Mississippi River. Within this parish and near the town of Vacherie is a no longer functioning sugar cane plantation called Rosepoint, inhabited primarily by black, English-speaking Louisianans. At the present time Rosepoint is not a sugar cane plantation but a community with recognizable boundaries and an *esprit de corps*.

The field work here described began in September, 1968, and continued through May, 1969, with less frequent visits during the following year. It was supported at various stages by the National Institute of Health, the National Institute of Mental Health, and the Tulane University Department of Anthropology. Their financial support is gratefully acknowledged.

An important stimulation for this work is the methodology called the "ethnography of communication" or the "ethnography of speaking." The aim of this approach is

> to investigate directly the use of language in contexts of situation so as to discern patterns proper to speech activity, patterns which escape separate studies of grammar, of personality, of religion, of kinship and the like, each abstracting from the patterning of speech activity as such into some other frame of reference. Secondly, such an approach cannot take linguistic form, a given code, or speech itself, as frame of reference. It must take as context a community, investigating its communicative habits as a whole, so that any given use of channel and code takes its place as but part of the resources upon which the members of the community draw (Hymes, 1964: 2–3).

The primary focus of such research is anthropological or ethnographic. What are the boundaries of the speech community? How do the people observed define and carry out situations requiring communication? In part this means focusing on concepts and situations which the community feels are somehow "real."

In the survey approach mothers are asked what they did or would do in raising their children. The experimental methodology tries to simulate conditions under which children might learn. The ethnographic approach, however, is to observe the ordinary, everyday interactions—in this case, child-rearing activities in the home. For example, in the speech act we call "disciplining," attention is paid to the participants, the witnesseses, the content of the messages, the method used for transmitting them, the frequency of this activity, and through subsequent inter-

1

views, the meanings attached to these activities. The linguistic analysis which might result from recording the speech act is secondary to the broader picture of what a child might learn from the experience about the nature of his world, that is, his family and community. It would seem probable that these language usages in child-rearing practices consciously or unconsciously predispose a child to certain patterns in the school or work situation. For this reason, we are concerned with

> what abilities the child must acquire beyond those of producing and interpreting all grammatical sentences in order to be a competent member of its community, knowing not only what may be said, but also what should and should not be said, and when and where (Hymes, 1964: 27).

As this study tries to indicate, the requirements of membership in a certain speech community vary with the social class or ethnicity of the community. In other words, the rules for language usage and effective speaking are not universal.

Two types of training for membership in a speech community are involved. The first is the entire belief system and philosophy which surrounds the rearing of children. This is illustrated in Rosepoint by the oft-heard statement "Them children worry my nerve," and the actions taken by the mother in accordance with this belief. It is possible to speak of a child-rearing tradition in Rosepoint, since the methods are handed down from mother to daughter. Dr. Spock, ladies' magazines, or popular trends in psychology have little currency here. This child-rearing philosophy forms a necessary background for language learning. The belief that children should be seen and not heard will determine the frequency if not the quality of interaction between children and adults. The choice of words, phrases, and the situations in which children are spoken to are all correlated with this philosophy.

The other type of language training is actual instruction in the forms of the language itself. In some cultures this would involve learning polite or honorific language; in others the "correct" choice of a particular noun or verb is emphasized. In certain segments of American society, it is commonly believed that parents have the responsibility of teaching their children "proper" grammatical forms as well as the etiquette of formal speech practices called "manners."

One of the major purposes of this research is to examine some of these real-life conditions under which children actually learn their language, how the families instill values about the use or nonuse of language, and how they use it in an everyday context. Some related theoretical issues are included for the reader's consideration, but that is secondary to the goal of describing communication habits and family interaction in the home environment of one community.

I want to show a specific example of cultural transmission. The conclusion is that the culture of Rosepoint is different from that of middle-class America and the forms of socialization (cultural transmission) may be so pervasive and strong in Rosepoint that subsequent exposures to American middle-class culture after the formative years are weak and ineffective by comparison. Educators, whose business is also cultural transmission, may want to make comparisons between the styles of this primary socialization described here and the forms of secondary socialization in the schools.

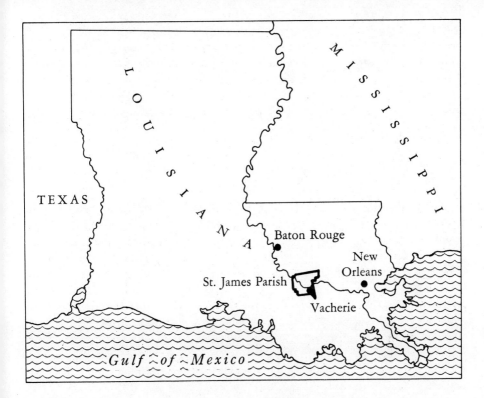

Map of Louisiana, showing the Vacherie area.

1 / The history and ethnographic background

Although there were white traders and opportunists recorded living among the Indians[1] in the Vacherie area by 1713 and possibly earlier, the first plantations were established about 1765. The first owners were actually homesteaders holding land grants from the French government. They came from France via New Orleans and in the next generation became landed gentry referred to as "Creoles."[2] The location of these land grants is still an important factor in the present settlement and land distribution patterns. The royal grants specified no more than 8 arpents fronting the river and 40 arpents[3] extending back in depth. Such plantations bordered the entire Mississippi in this area but behind *les quarantes* or 40 arpents, smaller farms and land holdings, not governable by the grants, were possible.

The Creoles built their houses adjacent to the Mississippi and donated land for churches, cemeteries, and schools. Under the conditions of the land grant, the land holders were required to build and maintain a levee to prevent flooding and a public road across the Mississippi front of their property (Bourgeois 1957: 18–37). In effect, this concentrated all settlement at the head of the property on the river. Of course, where the masters built their homes, the slaves were also housed. Everyone lived along the Mississippi where the land was richer and higher as a result of repeated flooding.

At Vacherie this settlement pattern had interesting results. In 1766 the Acadians arrived from Nova Scotia, and St. James Parish became known as "the First Acadian Coast" (Coulon 1967:7). Being of peasant ancestry and poor exiles to boot, the "Cajuns," as they have become known, settled on small farms behind the planta-

---

[1] Disease and culture contact had taken a heavy toll of the resident Indian tribes of the area: the Houma, Chitimacha, Alabama and other former tribes. The French census of 1769 lists only remnants of these groups (Bourgeois 1957:1).

[2] The term "Creole" has complex meanings in Louisiana. For examples of its historical meaning in St. James Parish, see Dufour (1967:116) or Bourgeois (1957:11–15, 26–37). In these instances Creole means the rich, educated, Frenchmen with land grants from the King of France rather than the peasant-derived, Nova Scotian exiles referred to as Acadians or Cajuns. Today, in popular usage, the term Creole is commonly employed to indicate anyone, black or white, with a French cultural heritage. The word also indicates parts of the cultural inventory believed to be of French derivation such as architectural styles, a type of tomato, or funeral customs.

[3] An arpent is slightly less than an acre and remains the unit of land measure in the parish today. The most thorough and reliable history of the region was written by a native son of St. James Parish, Alcée Fortier (1904; 4 vols.).

tions. This is the origin of Back Vacherie (present residents prefer the term South Vacherie). Between the Great River Road settlements and the Cajun community several miles back from the river are only sugar cane fields.

Recently, a narrow strip of businesses and homes only one lot thick on each side of the "New Vacherie Road" connects back and front Vacherie. This thin, broken strip of settlement backed up to the sugar cane fields has become the "civic center" of town. Stretched along these several miles are the Post Office, the bank, utilities such as gas, water, electricity, railroad station, branch library, Office of Economic Opportunity, and assorted businesses. No place in Vacherie, with the possible exception of a Cajun restaurant, can be considered the heart of town. It is interesting to compare this completely dispersed settlement pattern dominated by a great river with the Spanish plaza or the English village square system.

While the big plantations cultivated indigo and, after the turn of the century, cotton and sugar cane, the Acadians raised rice, tobacco, corn, hay, fruit, and pecans. They herded cattle, poultry, and swine, hunted game, fished the bayous, and gathered moss and roots. Vacherie was settled almost entirely by French speakers, and until the 1940s French was the only language spoken in the schools and churches. Today much of the community is bilingual, though more French is used in Back Vacherie.

In 1769 this region was ceded to Spain and ceded back to France in 1800. As it took three years for news of the latter transfer to reach St. James Parish, the residents had only twenty days to enjoy renewed French citizenship before word of the Louisiana Purchase arrived. This marks the end of the colonial period and the beginning of an era of the very large and very rich sugar cane plantations. These were the golden years of the French Creole culture: mansions, riverboats, *ce grande monde, haut couture,* and slaves. Naturally, all this ended abruptly with the Civil War.

The century following 1860 was an economic disaster from which the area has only now begun to recover. Land changed hands many times, though the borders remained fairly fixed. Much land went uncultivated and yielded only a narrow margin of profit (Dufour 1967:175). The old-fashioned techniques of sugar production necessitated a large unskilled labor force. This labor force, overwhelmingly black, continued to live on the plantations for which they worked. Houses were provided, the company store on the front of the property sold the basic necessities, and the owner or manager took care of other problems. It is only within the past decade that jobs and training for the unskilled have been available and these are outside the parish.

Thus the plantation system still exists, *de facto* if not *de jure.* The boundaries of the old land grants, more or less intact, are well known to the local people. Frequently, instead of address or birth places only the name of the plantation is used. Many families can number three or four generations who have spent their lives on that land. The plantation boundaries are adhered to even when the plantation itself is no longer a functioning economic unit. This is the case with Rosepoint and Laurel Plantations. Even though the land has been subdivided and now is owned by many individuals, the area is always identified as such-and-such a plantation.

ROSEPOINT

Plantations such as St. Joseph ("San Jo"), St. James, and St. Amant are productive economic units whose residents feel a sense of geographical and ethnic identification. They are genuine sugar cane plantations and those who live within their boundaries are full time employees. When sugar cane harvesting or "grinding," milling, and planting are completed, the plantation vegetable gardens are cultivated. In return for this, the owners of the plantation provide a house, a local store, and an ever decreasing amount of the paternalistic benefits associated with plantation life. This system can, of course, become unmanageable and then the land on which the houses are built is subdivided and sold and the labor is recruited from an open market.

Such an area is Rosepoint. Formerly a plantation, the land has been subdivided and sold. The section along the Mississippi contains the old, two-room, shotgun style houses, company stores now privately owned, and the newly built contract houses.

On the north side flows the Mississippi River, whose waters are hidden from view by high levees. On the south side of Rosepoint the Texas and Pacific Rail-

A plantation, complete with manor house on the right, company store on the left, and cane growing in the field.

road tracks separate homes from fields. Sugar cane fields adjoin Rosepoint at its eastern and western sides.

The winding road at the foot of the levee is the only public face of Rosepoint. "The front," as local residents call the stores that line the highway, is all a visitor would see of Rosepoint. The six lanes are perpendicular to the river road. Because they end at the railroad tracks and have no other intersections, one would not "pass down the lane" without specific business. A tiny turnaround is provided at the railroad track end and one returns back down the lane to go to any other lane. This arrangement, while not planned, gives the residents privacy and an opportunity to scrutinize traffic.

Thus Rosepoint is not shaped like a suburb with "blocks" and streets which give access to other streets. Reflecting its plantation origin, it has a "front" where the manor house on the river stood at one time and where stores and churches now stand, and a "back," a former place of slave quarters and now of small homes. These boundaries have no political or legal significance and would not show up on any map as a borough or municipality. However, for the local residents these dividing lines have an immediate and compelling reality. The major elements of their community lives are enclosed here: the grade school and junior high school, the town meeting hall, the neighborhood food and general stores, the two Baptist churches, the cemetery, two bars, a filling station, a beauty shop, and a lumber market. The churches, cemetery, and town hall were built and are maintained by volunteer labor. "Here in Rosepoint . . ." "In Rosepoint we do . . ." "The people of Rosepoint think . . ." are frequent phrases. The question "where were you born" usually elicits the name of a plantation, particularly from older people.

The various "ball clubs," which annually sponsor a costumed dance, are composed of blacks from these plantations. Originally a pre-Lenten observance, the dances are sometimes held in the summer now. The Rosepoint Pleasure Club, the Lords and Ladies Pleasure Club and others, although founded on separate plantations, now have members scattered throughout Vacherie. These banquet-dances are financed through a series of "hops" to which the community contributes food and pays admission. All children (that is, those not of marriageable age) are excluded from the festivities.

In addition to the ball clubs a large number of voluntary societies function as social service organizations. An example is the Young Soldiers' Benevolent Association whose purpose is to pay the bills for a doctor's house calls. Since visits to the doctor's office are not covered, one sick man had to be smuggled to the doctor on the floor of the car. This was a necessary measure if he hoped to collect; too many people in Rosepoint have sharp eyes.

The Rosepoint Mutual Aid Benevolent Society is primarily a burial society with strong ties to the local Baptist churches. Designed to insure that all members receive a well-attended, proper burial, the Society fines members who do not attend other members' funerals. Yearly dues provide the operating expenses. New members pay five dollars to join, fifty cents per month, and a dollar for every funeral missed.

Many families in Rosepoint count four living generations and remember sev-

Another lane.

eral past generations of families who have owned property there. Some families lived on the land when it was a producing plantation as well as later when the land was sold to individuals. Many others, however, have lived here only in their lifetime, usually having come from a producing plantation where they had somewhat the status of indentured servants. Frequently a girl marries a man off her plantation. With the help of the family they save their money, pool their resources, and buy or rent a lot in Rosepoint. With this base the couple provides a half-way house for relatives to break the plantation habit.

The case of Emilie Macdonald is typical of ties between those who live in Rosepoint and those who live in other parts of Vacherie. Emilie lives in a rented house in Rosepoint and supports her invalid husband, eight children and grandchildren with a job obtained through the Poverty Program. Formerly she cut cane. Four of her brothers and sisters live in the Parish.

One brother is employed in heavy industry. His wife and three children live in Back Vacherie. A second brother, likewise employed in heavy industry, lives in Rosepoint with his wife and seven children. They have built a home on a plot of ground owned by his wife's extended family. Her third brother is seasonally employed as a canecutter but lives in a rented house in Rosepoint. Her sister and her sister's husband are canecutters who live in a plantation provided housing on a producing plantation a mile up the river from Rosepoint.

THE INFLUENCE OF TRANSPLANTED FRENCH CULTURE

The Vacherie area was settled almost exclusively by French people, the "Cajuns" exiled from Nova Scotia and those from the rich, landed families of France. Courthouse records show how a German peasant population was quickly absorbed with the Old Country names of Schoen, Edelmaier, Weber, Vogel, and Zweig becoming the New Country French names of Chaigne, Delmaire, Vebre, Fauquel and Labranche (Dufour 1967:82). The only other non-French population was the slaves. Of their assimilation no record exists. The census of 1766 claims 266 whites and 16 slaves; by 1950 the white population was 285 and the black population was 7833 (Bourgeois 1957:202). Today the population is split half and half.[4]

Although most of the black men and women fifty and older speak French, very few of the children do. White children far more frequently speak French at home. The Office of Economic Opportunity reports that several very rural black families still speak only French. The rest are bilingual or monolingual. At any rate, French as a language, first or second, has been maintained with less frequency in black families than in white. This may in part be due to the lack of identification with French culture or to segregated schools. Those who do not speak French believe that others use it to keep secrets and hold discussions without being understood.

Although it is possible to demonstrate in many minor ways the still vital influence of French culture of the eighteenth century, the two most telling remnants of France are cooking and religion.

Life magazine has called Cajun cooking "a culinary artistry that is perhaps the finest French provincial cuisine to be found anywhere. It is a blend of traditional French cooking with the cuisine of Spanish colonizers and utilizes secrets acquired from Indians and Africans" (Snell 1969:188). There are many good books written on the art of Cajun cooking. In January or during any convenient cold spell comes *la boucherie* (the hog killing) from which comes *boudin blanc et boudin rouge* (white and red sausage), *l'andouille*, and other pork delicacies. Pigpens and giant boiling pots are a common sight. Few in the community serve anything but rice, beans, pork, seafood, chicken, and vegetables fixed in this traditional manner.

In St. James Parish there are only two routes to salvation: the Catholic and the Baptist. In the 1960 census only forty-five out of 18,000 people listed their religion as other than Baptist or Catholic. The Catholics outnumber the Baptists by eight to one, though by not so great a margin among blacks. The theological tensions which might normally be assumed to exist between so disparate a twosome, in fact, do not exist. In a fascinating case of religious syncretism the Baptists have taken unto themselves some of the characteristics of Catholicism. They have in-

---

[4] U.S. Department of Commerce, Bureau of the Census, *United States Census of Population: 1960*, Vol. I, *Characteristics of the Population*, part 20, Louisiana, Table 27, page 86.

fant baptism (or christening), the Douay version of the Bible, strict Lenten observances, catchechism classes, crucifixes, Saint's day remembrances, and plastic statues of the Holy Family and saints. In addition the Baptists practice adult baptism—until two years ago in the Mississippi River—and public confession of sins. The Catholic Church is outside Rosepoint and supported by the Diocese, while the three smaller Baptist churches are within Rosepoint and supported by members of the congregation.

All, regardless of religious affiliation, observe burial practices which in the heyday of French culture reached epic proportions. Today elaborate funeral services, wakes, and *La Toussaint* are all that remain; the extended mourning requirements have faded and the poor cannot afford marble monuments. Wakes are the central part of the funeral. Relatives and friends maintain an all-night vigil, view the body, burn candles, eat the food contributed, discuss the departed and the circumstances of his demise. Attendance at a wake allows more identification with the family, display of emotion, and concrete assistance than does funeral attendance. On November 1, *le jour des Morts*, or All Saints' Day, the cemeteries are cleaned, the tombs whitewashed, and flowers placed. In Rosepoint the cemetery is located just the other side of the railroad tracks, and is the only part of the community so separated. Most people expressed an active dislike for going to the cemetery at any time other than All Saints' Day, but that day is special. School is out, and there is much laughing and feasting.

At the other end of life—birth—there are also French influences. Shortly after the baby's birth all the relatives and friends are summoned and a service in the church is held for the baby. The main result of a christening is to equip the child with a *parain*[5] or godparent. The *parain* is usually an aunt or uncle of the newborn, perhaps a distant one, or a cousin. This practice is, as in the case of the Mexican *comadre* or *compadre* relationship, a serious undertaking for anyone and a matter of some importance to the child. The theological reason, expressed in the service, is to give the child, sinful and unsaved, a spiritual counselor and teacher. In "folk reinterpretation" a *parain* is responsible for giving a Christmas present or for contributing, in case of need, a pair of shoes, a party dress, or petty cash. Moreover, the *parain* will assume responsibility for the child in the event of some family disaster—a duty seldom fulfilled.

For the child a *parain* is somebody who probably has fewer godchildren than his own parents have children and whose attentions and pocketbook might be monopolized. One of the most frequent conversations among children is about the relative value of their *parains*. All children are born with one, so to speak, but through death, mobility, or indifference they may lose this right.

Weddings in the Catholic Church, as distinguished from Baptist or civil ceremonies, must be marked by some indication of the bride's status—virgin or not. If not, she must wear some article of color on her person: a handkerchief, shoes,

---

[5] The term *parain* comes from the French word for godfather, *parrain*. In the New World French usage the spelling is changed, and the Louisiana word *parain* usually means both godfather and godmother. (The French word for godmother, *marraine*, is rarely used in Louisiana.) If the child's aunt, uncle, or cousin is chosen, the relative may be from either the mother's or the father's side of the family.

belt, or anything colorful. This sanction is enforced by the priest and public opinion—the already certain knowledge of the community. All of the Catholic women spoke quite frankly about this custom and their degree of participation. As most of them had been married ten to fifteen years ago, it is difficult to determine if this custom is declining or is the result of a particular priest's idiosyncrasies. Just as there is little or no social opprobrium for unwed mothers, there is little or none for the more colorful brides.

Despite the incorporation of these French customs, vocabulary items, or Cajun intonation patterns, the blacks of St. James Parish probably have more in common with their tenant farmer, unskilled laborer counterparts in Mississippi and Alabama. The identity is with the ex-slave black population of the South rather than with the ex-French white population of Louisiana.

BLACK AND WHITE RELATIONSHIPS

The violence and hostility beneath the surface of racial relations in many southern areas are less conspicuous here. During the presidential elections of November, 1968, St. James was one of four parishes in Louisiana to vote for Hubert Humphrey. Other parishes favored George Wallace. Local black politicians and businessmen in St. James regard the "easygoing" people of the predominantly French area of southern Louisiana as more congenial than the "red-necks" in northern Louisiana or Mississippi. Perhaps associated with this more tolerant attitude is the long-standing historical tradition in the New Orleans area of educated, landed, Free People of Color, in one sense a black aristocracy.

Nevertheless, this is not intended as a compliment to racial harmony. Whites of this parish have, as elsewhere in the South, tried many tactics to preserve a segregated school system. Despite the reluctance of local whites, voter registration, restaurants, some jobs, and housing opportunities have opened to black residents. The myths of southern race relations have been retained along with such verbal buttresses to segregation as differential use of names and titles.

The most damaging form of discrimination is economic. The job situation for laborers—low pay, difficult or dangerous work, rampant paternalism, and seasonal unemployment—duplicates in this sugarcane producing area the same facts so well documented for the cotton producing areas of the South. It is still easier for poor rural whites to leave the two-room shotgun style house and other realities of poverty behind them than it is for the black family. Furthermore, those who do leave the country fare little better in the crowded city. The possibility of a better job must be weighed against the loss of the supportive kindred, the higher cost of living, and the problems which beset city dwellers.

2 / The ethnographic methodology

NATALIE: Come on sit on the chair. Sit on the chair. Peter, sit on the chair. What you want ask that lady? Get up and ask Joan what you want. Her name is Joan. Now come ask her what you want ask her. You want to ask who that baby for in her arms?

PETER: Where?

NATALIE: That baby what she holding.

PETER: Yeah.

NATALIE: Well ask her!!

PETER: [*Moans*] ———.

NATALIE: Get up and ask her!! STAND UP!

PETER: [*Intimidated whisper*] That your baby?

NATALIE: *STAND UP PETER!!*

PETER: [*Desperate*] That your baby?

INVESTIGATOR: No, this is Pearl's baby. This is Susie.

PETER: [*Whispers*] Oh.

NATALIE: Answer her.

INVESTIGATOR: You know Pearl?

PETER: Hunh?

INVESTIGATOR: You know Pearl?

PETER: Yeah.

Seven Rosepoint homes were visited and intensive observations of the children in these homes were made for the purpose of studying their acquisition of language in their own habitat. In these seven homes, informal interviews, participant observations, and tape recordings were conducted at weekly intervals. It was possible to spend the night with one of the seven families. Such occasions and weekend visits were the only chance to observe the fathers and adult men.

Since only two out of the seven households had automobiles, offering needed transportation repaid kindnesses and served for many data-collecting purposes. The absence of a room or office from which to operate was a serious handicap for which the car did not fully compensate.

Technological sophistication was represented by a Uher 4000 Reporter. Although this tape recorder was in constant evidence, obtaining a good recording was virtually impossible. The noice level of these homes, even at quieter moments, violated the auditory requirements for successful taping. At the investigator's suggestion, the television and the phonograph were turned off (an unnatural situation). As we waited for the whining cycle of the washing machine to finish, a neighbor would drop by, the beans would boil, the cane trucks rumble, and the children lose interest. Adequate recording conditions were never attained. More-over, obtaining an approximation of good acoustic conditions meant creating such an artificial social atmosphere that spontaneity was hampered. The various means used to elicit speech will later be introduced as evidence of language usage patterns. As an instrument of research, however, a tape recorder was only a necessary evil rather than an intrinsic aid.

The recorder was regarded throughout the study with suspicion. The women would frequently say, "Let me put that thing on top of the refrigerator," or "You don't need it." Usually at the first opportunity of separating researcher and re-corder, the recorder would be shut up in the back room. The adults were contin-ually afraid that the children would break it. Their reservations about the tape recorder contrasted with their willingness to confide anything to the investigator. With genuine openness they discussed their own and others' marital life, family relations, child-rearing practices, financial affairs, and local customs. After they resolved their initial bewilderment at the role of the investigator, there was no apparent attempt on their part to conceal information.

Ultimately the best research strategy was to take advantage of the complete access to these homes to participate in the daily routines, take notes, and ask questions when some occasion arose. Frequent, lengthy, and often unpredictable visits eliminated "staging" or company manners. After the introductory period, life went on as usual. At any rate, the major tool of this research is the day by day, month by month familiarity of close contact which breeds a certain intuition. This "feel" can then be assessed in the light of more sophisticated methods and theories.

The section of transcript at the beginning of the chapter comes from a tape taken November 11, 1968. Present for the taping sessions are Natalie Powell, her adult daughter Lizabeth, Lizabeth's daughter Anne, aged three, and Natalie's youngest sons, three and ten months. These boys, Fortrel and Scott, are Liz's brothers and Anne's uncles. Other children, Susie and Peter, have accompanied the investigator.

Throughout the tape, the adults are seated around the kitchen table and the children range through the room and the adjoining living room. Since the floors and ceilings are plaster, and the tables, chairs, curtains, and upholstery are plastic, there is nothing to absorb the sound; hence, echoes are bad. Neighbors enter and leave. Because there was no attempt to structure the conversation, several are going at once. Nonetheless, this is the optimal, spontaneous recording situation for the community.

THE CHILDREN'S REACTIONS AS DATA

As has been suggested by the ethnomethodologists Sachs and Garfinkel (1969), even the failure to obtain so-called hard facts should be introduced as evidence. That information about speech and language style is unavailable because of local attitudes or a quirk of social structure is in itself an important observation, quite likely missed in the typical interview situation. What a given person refuses to

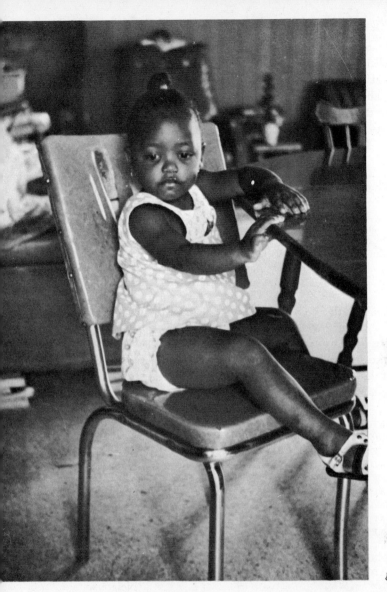

*A good baby
going visiting.*

say, when, and why, is as much a part of the data as is a fairly predictable standard answer.[1]

For the first two months of this project attempts to elicit spontaneous speech
from the children met with defeat, with or without the tape recorder. The readiness
to show off, the constant flow of speech, and the mother-child interaction so common in middle-class children were nowhere in evidence. The children appeared
to speak as little to their parents as to the investigator. One twenty-eight-month
male spoke three words in as many months. Meanwhile, the mothers claimed that
the verbal precocity of their children was driving them up the wall.

---

[1] The introduction of Evans-Pritchard's *The Nuer* (1967:1–16) also illustrates this
problem.

The initial taping session for each of the families was a free-for-all. The intention was to elicit spontaneous child-to-child speech and adult-to-child speech as well as to break the ice and to accustom the families to the presence of a tape recorder. Oh, idle dreams. The following is a partial transcript of a tape taken at the home of the maternal aunt of a Rosepoint family. Five adults and ten children, ages two to twelve, were present.

> MOTHER: Where you go? Tell Joan where you went, Desiree. Desiree! Desiree!! DESIREE! *DESIREE!* Tell Joan where you went. [*Volunteers*] In the graveyard.
> OLDER STRAY CHILD: No, the state fair.
> MOTHER: [*addressing her niece*] Nicki, where you went? Get your finger out of your nose! Where you go? Nicki! NICKI! NICKI! That's why you ain't going to no game tonight. I ain't taking her nowhere. Desiree, you ain't going to no game if you don't tell me where you went.
> DESIREE: [*The child remains silent.*]
> MOTHER: You show Joan how you can dance. [*Switches on radio.*]

This is the most talkative child and well-educated mother in the sample.

In the next few taping sessions canned materials were tried. The idea of recording spontaneous speech was dropped temporarily in order to break the sound barrier. Sentence imitations, sentence completions and story retelling were used as much to evoke any segments as for the data they themselves could provide.[2] The following is a tape segment attempting sentence imitations.

> INVESTIGATOR: [*An explanation of how to play this game has preceded. The child is four.*] Can you say 'Is that a fire truck?'
> MADELAINE: [*Nods.*]
> INVESTIGATOR: Can you say the sentence? Can you say 'Is that a fire truck?'
> MADELAINE: [*Nods.*]
> INVESTIGATOR: Okay.
> MADELAINE: That's a fire truck.
> INVESTIGATOR: That's good. Can you say 'We go to the store tomorrow?'
> MADELAINE: Yes.
> INVESTIGATOR: Okay, say it.
> MADELAINE: Go to store tomorrow.
> INVESTIGATOR: Now I am older.
> MADELAINE: [*Stares.*]
> INVESTIGATOR: Can you say 'Now I am older?'
> MADELAINE: [*With difficulty*] Now I am older.

From the remainder of the tape one receives the impression that few if any of these sentences are native or familiar to this child. She imitated with great awkwardness but made only minor syntactic errors. Her female cousin, age three, made fewer errors and imitated with no visible difficulty. Two boys, aged two

---

[2] The sentence completions and imitations were taken from Slobin et al., (1967:194, 206). The stories to be retold by the children were adapted from Alcée Fortier (1895), a famous Louisiana storyteller who collected the Jean Sot (Silly John) tales from the Vacherie area blacks. As the children were unreceptive to any story retelling endeavors, the search for culture free tales was irrelevant.

and a half and five, tried several sentences before deciding to abandon the project. None of the other males were even this cooperative. Moreover, boys are extremely difficult to understand off tape as well as on. (Why, I don't know.)

Unfortunately, for the sentence completions the pattern of our little game had been set.

> INVESTIGATOR: [*An explanation of how to play has preceded. The child is to complete the sentence.*] I have a bag of candy and
> CHILD: I have a bag of candy and
> INVESTIGATOR: And what? What about your bag of candy?
> CHILD: What about your bag of candy? [*Tape*]

Local folk tales had no better reception. Preceding this segment is the first reading of the tale, and a request for comprehension and retelling. Several interruptions and general lack of response necessitate retelling the tale.

> INVESTIGATOR: I'm going to read you a story. About Foolish John or Silly John.
> MADELAINE: Foolish John.
> KENNETH: [*Her brother, thirty-four months old*] What this?
> SPENCER: [*Eleven year old sister*] Kenneth, that's you. [*She means he is foolish. She addresses Madelaine.*] Tell her what she tell you about when she finish reading.
> INVESTIGATOR: Foolish John's mother told him to put pepper in the gumbo.
> KENNETH: What this?
> INVESTIGATOR: Now what did Foolish John's mother tell Foolish John?
> KENNETH: What this is?
> MOTHER: What she tell him to do, Madelaine?
> MADELAINE: [*No answer.*]
> INVESTIGATOR: She told him to put pepper in the gumbo.
> MOTHER: Now listen good and you gonna hear what she say.
> INVESTIGATOR: Now Foolish John had a dog named Pepper.
> MADELAINE: Foolish John had a dog named Pepper.
> INVESTIGATOR: Now what's going to happen—can you tell me?
> MADELAINE: [*Silence.*]
> INVESTIGATOR: What kind of pepper did the mother mean?
> MADELAINE: [*Silence.*]
> INVESTIGATOR: The kind that goes with salt, right?
> MADELAINE: [*Silence.*]
> INVESTIGATOR: But Foolish John who's stupid picked up his dog Pepper and threw him in.
> MADELAINE: Yeah.

Attempting the same procedure with others netted no better results. Kenneth says 'What this?' and other variations forty-nine times on this tape. He is examining a seed catalogue and could not be less interested in other games. The questions did result in an interesting game with him later. When children eight to eleven were asked for stories, they told *Jack and the Beanstalk*, *The Three Little Pigs*, and *Cinderella*.

Throughout these taping sessions there was an attempt to create conversational openings for the children. Asking middle-class children a direct question is the equivalent of giving them the floor. They then have permission, so to speak, to talk at will. An adult's question or comment or even recognition of their presence validates the right to a stream of speech. Many investigators have encountered a willingness in middle-class children to talk freely. Frequently these garrulous children are not easily discouraged or shut off.

> There were those who warned that the child would be shy and speechless in our presence; this was not the case . . . We were eagerly welcomed, shown a parade of toys and games, and talked to rather steadily (Brown and Fraser 1964:51).

It is appropriate here to note that conversational openers and questions, such as are commonly used in American classrooms, are not universals. A really well-phrased question rated a monosyllabic or in rare cases a trisyllablic answer. Most queries received an inexplicable dark-eyed stare or a shy grin and ducked head.

Some success must be reported. After some role in the community had been assigned to the investigator by the children, the first two months of silence gave way to limited conversation and even volunteered information—not the extensive corpus we had anticipated, but gratifying. However, the failure of the formal elicitation methods ultimately demonstrates some features about language usage in this community. It was naive to assume that a corpus adequate enough for a syntactic analysis of spontaneous speech, input, and language acquisition could be obtained from this setting. The requirements are too unnatural. Therein, however, lies a rich source of information.

3 / The family of them children

NATALIE: You right there because them children be bad. Now who gonna talk.

LIZ: Anne, you all ready? Anne and them might not want to talk. Fortrel, you want to talk first, eh? What's you all gonna say? Anything special?

FORTREL: *Yeah.* [*Everyone laughs heartily.*]

NATALIE: [*Still laughing*] Fortrel he say yeah.

LIZ: Them children is something.

NATALIE: And where your Daddy?

PETER: To work.

NATALIE: And where your Mama?

PETER: To home.

NATALIE: Un-hunh.

PETER: To home.

NATALIE: Home?

PETER: Mama to Uncle Jim.

NATALIE: Oh, your mama to Uncle Jim? Un-hunh.

FAMILY "LIFE-SPACE" AND COMPOSITION

Any description of the child's acquisition of communicative competence begins with his "life-space," that is, the physical environment and the individuals who make up his network of interaction. The seven families studied are described in this manner below.

Family One   The working husband, a wife and eight children ages two and a half to twelve were all born in Rosepoint. The mother was married at age fifteen; the father was then twenty-one. The youngest child, a male, has lived with the husband's sister's family since he was five months old. While he knows his real parents and says the appropriate kinship terms, he prefers his aunt's house. During the cane cutting season, while the aunt is seasonally employed, the boy stays with his mother and she returns him after working hours. The arrangement is easy and congenial. Both the aunt and the mother joke about the child receiving the best of the two families. The only other son in the family is the third child, aged nine.

The oldest and the two youngest daughters share one bed. All the middle children, three girls and a boy, share another double bed. Although the contract house has four bedrooms, the children will not spread out to occupy the fourth bedroom for fear of ghosts. They like closeness, having grown up in a two-room house. The baby, who lives with his aunt, sleeps with his two teenage female cousins.

Family Two   This household is composed of a working husband, a wife, five children, and the wife's uncle. The children include four boys, nine, seven, four, and two, and a girl, five. The wife's uncle, a permanent household member, is the youngest son of her grandmother, who raised her. The wife feels she is repaying her debt to her grandmother by taking care of the last baby. Actually the wife and the uncle are close to the same age and were raised as brother and sister. He is semiemployed, very quiet, has never married, and will babysit for the children when asked. He does not live with his sister (who is the wife's mother up the street) because hers is only a two room house.

Another semipermanent member of the family is the wife's nephew, age six. His mother lives in Marrero, a small town about forty miles from Vacherie, and the child divides his time between his aunt's house and his grandmother's, two doors down. The family as a whole is responsible for this boy's rearing. The oldest son in this house spend most nights and all weekends with his grandmother, who is raising him. He stays with his mother only when his grandmother is at work.

The house is a six-room contract house. The daughter has one bedroom, the uncle another, and the couple the last one. The boys rotate among these three double beds and a rollaway bed in the living room. Sometimes there are five boys to be distributed, at other times only three.

Family Three   This family unit consists of an employed husband, a wife, seven children, and one grandchild. This grandchild, three, is the baby of the eldest daughter, twenty-one, who dropped out of school when she became pregnant. She raised her own daughter and her little brother, both three years old, because her mother was temporarily employed as a cook. Later the mother quit her cooking job at the Cajun restaurant (which has belonged to the family for twenty years and passes from woman to woman) to give birth to a child now a year old. The family has completely accepted the grandchild and regards her as one of their own. The eldest daughter has serious child-rearing responsibilities for all the younger children, hers included.

In the spring of 1969, the seventeen-year-old daughter was be the first in her family to graduate from high school. Three of the sons suffer from congenital heart defects.

Theirs is a six-room contract house. All the girls, twenty-one, seventeen, and three, sleep in the middle bedroom. The boys, sixteen, fifteen, twelve, and three, occupy the last bedroom.

Family Four   The mother is on relief. She has fourteen children, twelve now living, eight of these within Rosepoint. Still at home with her are a twelve-year-old son and sixteen-year-old daughter with her own daughter aged fourteen months. Two of the grown sons divide their time between this house and their grandmother's (the mother's mother) one-half block away.

The father of this large family lives with his girlfriend three blocks away, works at a white-owned local business, and contributes cash on demand to his children and numerous grandchildren. Two boys are high school graduates; one is a freshman in college. The grandmother, who cannot read or write, is a unifying influence on the family.

The house is a four-room shotgun, extremely crowded but clean. Sleeping arrangements are fluid. Generally the mother sleeps in the front bedroom, the daughter and granddaughter in the second, and all the sons in the living room containing two single beds and a double. Miscellaneous children and grandchildren spend the night frequently. This dwelling, like the other shotguns, rents for twenty-five dollars a month.

Family Five In this three-room shotgun with no bath live the working mother, her semiemployed boyfriend, her four children and her adult brother. While the mother works the brother cooks, washes, and babysits for the children, twelve, eleven, nine, and three. The nine year old is the only son.

The little three-year-old girl is as independent as she is unsupervised. She decides at which neighbor's or relative's home she will eat and sleep, and she can be found during the day anywhere from the local stores to the levee.

Waiting for their grandmother on the porch of a shotgun.

Family Six   Living in this larger than average shotgun is the wife, her husband, her mother, and her three children, eight, six, and three. The mother divorced her first husband and has recently celebrated the first anniversary of her second marriage. Her second husband has assumed the responsibility of caring for her three children by her first marriage. They are a devoted couple.

The wife is a high school graduate. The husband has an excellent job at a local chemical plant thirty miles away. The wife's mother is a professional housekeeper, who lived in California for a period and has several children who have upwardly mobile, white-collar jobs such as dietician and teacher. One is married to a doctor. The grandmother owns the house and is indisputably in charge.

The children spend much of their time with the mother's sister next door, who has ten children aged two to twenty. The three-year-old girl is a hyperactive child, but clearly the brightest around. Her alertness leads her into constant conflict with her mother and grandmother.

Family Seven   This family lives in a four room shotgun, which has no bathroom, and when the bills are not paid, no electricity or running water. The father is usually unemployed and is regarded generally by the community as a "no-good." When he has been idle for a long stretch, the mother takes the children, a girl aged five and a boy, two, and "leaves" him, that is, she goes home to her mother, who lives in a trailer parked on the back of the lot. He views this as desertion and mopes about.

When the mother is living at home, her children sleep together in their bedroom. At her mother's trailer, however, they mingle with approximately twelve others.

Not only the grandmother but two sisters, three aunts, and uncounted cousins, nieces, and nephews live in nearby houses where children are welcome at any time. One of the sisters, the only high school graduate in the family, is an industrious college student with two children, a newborn and a year-old baby.

CHARACTERISTICS OF THE HOUSEHOLD

All of these families share important structural and demographic features. Only one of these families is nuclear, that is, composed solely of father, mother and only the children born to them. Most have three generations, or extra siblings, nieces, or nephews, present. Two families have daughters whose own children have been incorporated into the household. The mother of family five has also offered to accept the children of her son.

The proximity to relatives and their mutual sharing must be emphasized. All of the households have at least three other families of close kin within one minute's walk. Many elements of a common life are shared: child care duties, cooking chores, money, land, beds, and the last bean in the pot. This sharing mitigates the low standard of living afforded by relief checks and allows some luxuries for those living at subsistence level. Moreover, women are not isolated with their children day after day. The task of raising five children is greatly simplified when they can be distributed easily throughout the neighborhood. Some extended families own their land in common and build homes adjacent to each other. Baby clothes, kitchen utensils, food, cash windfalls, and luxuries like electric mixers or vacuum cleaners are owned by joint families.

No child observed sleeps in a room alone. The average occupancy rate is about three children per room. Children are not segregated into beds strictly on the basis of sex and age but rather on the basis of compatibility and the number of beds available. Since there are always loose children to be parceled out at bedtime, adults rarely sleep alone. Double beds with only one adult occupant are much too inviting.

All of the families now live or have within the past three years lived in shotguns, the unpainted, crowded, esthetically unappealing wooden houses which so characterize the life of the southern black. Built from the scraps of older houses, the rooms of shotguns are arranged one after the other without halls. (See Diagram 1 for a standard design.) They contain, typically, two, three, or four rooms straight back, a front porch, sometimes with bath or extra rooms added onto the sides of the original house. What may have been the outside of another house becomes the bedroom walls of a shotgun. Windows are not made to fit or doors to hang properly. As closets are not included in construction, cedar closets or "chiffon robes" must be purchased for clothes. These bulky wardrobes consume so much space that living space is cramped. In a shotgun every room is a bedroom. In the Vacherie area a two room shotgun, often housing a family of ten, rents for twenty to thirty dollars per month.

Diagram 1. A typical "shotgun."

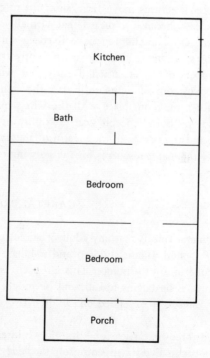

An increase in jobs for blacks at Avondale Shipping Yard and local chemical plants has allowed some of the families to move into contract houses. These are cheaply constructed, preassembled frame houses with a standard floor plan for each price. Three bedrooms, a living room, dining room and bath represent a material improvement over shotguns (See Diagram 2). However, within two years they begin to deteriorate visibly. They are as shoddily constructed as the law will permit. Furthermore, the high interest rate and carrying charges on a thirty year loan vitiate the ostensibly low prices. The average monthly payment for a contract house is one hundred dollars; the lot on which it is built costs one thousand dollars. Recently some residents have moved into house trailers.

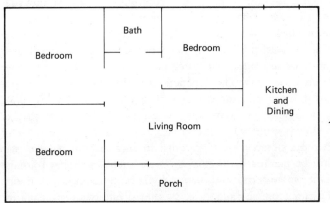

Diagram 2.
A typical "contract."

The recency of this move from shotguns to contract houses and trailers should be emphasized because it means that virtually all people in Rosepoint including the current crop of children have lived in small houses of four rooms or less. Renters of shotguns tend to move frequently from one such dwelling to another. Home owners move less often. Family One with their eight children lived in a series of two-room shotguns until after the eighth baby was walking. Family Two stayed in a three-room place with the wife's mother, sister and brother until the fifth child was born. The physical proximity of the houses, the nearness of many relatives, and the person-to-room ratio of the dwelling afford little privacy. *People* are one of the major resources for the growing child.

CARETAKERS

The general rule is that any adult or adolescent child is responsible for and can "mind" the child. Infant children and toddlers in particular are cuddled and held by everyone in arms' distance. This affect tends to diminish as the child ceases to be a baby. As he begins to talk and be independent, he becomes a fixture. Little effort or interest is expended on children two and older. Such children are omnipresent.

By age three or earlier for boys, the children are included in peer groups and travel in packs. Every happening on the lane is attended by these children, who spend a large part of each day traversing well-worn paths between the store, favorite relatives, and home.

Caretaking responsibilities are extended without question to any person within disciplining distance of the child. Friends, relatives, and neighbors share in the management of children. Since the children spend much time at the homes of adults other than their parents, there is as little hesitation at whacking or yelling at another's child as at one's own. This is done with equal ease in front of the child's parents and is regarded as fair and just. There is, in other words, no jealous guarding of the exclusive parental prerogative of caretaking. Mothers may engage in arguments with their friends and relatives on whether frequent punishment and hard work are good for children, but there is never any discussion on *who* is responsible for their behavior. All are.

The pattern observed in many societies of relegating the care of the youngest to the next oldest is not institutionalized here. However, a basic principle of care-taking, the responsibility of the older for the younger, is a salient feature of the socialization process. Adolescents accept a generalized child-rearing burden for the younger children. In a family of six girls the three oldest girls, for example, undertake the daily task of brushing and braiding the hair of the three younger girls.

The older children also assist in dressing, feeding, tending, and more important, in teaching many of the social and intellectual skills traditionally learned in child-hood. Alphabets, colors, numbers, rhymes, word games, pen and pencil games are learned, *if at all*, from older children. No child, even the firstborn, is without such tutelage, since cousins, aunts, and uncles of their own age and older are always on hand.

Men cuddle, coo at, and carry on about babes-in-arms, but exert no maintenance *per se*—no feeding, dressing, putting to sleep, or entertaining. Frequently, remarks are heard on the desirability and delight of large families. One young man confided that he wanted twenty children!

AGE GRADING

The arbitrary divisions which a society makes within the growth process are called age grades and influence the treatment of individuals passing through each stage. The recognition and cultural definition of these maturational stages determine what kinds of language are addressed to the child. The stages of childhood, or age grades, in Rosepoint are as follows.

Babies From infancy to the time of yard walking and talking, a child is a baby. Babies are greatly desired. As noted above, the current youngest child is favored with constant attention, fed part of all choice food, and denied nothing. When no other children are forthcoming, this last child may be referred to as the "baby" for many years. One thirty-five-year-old man is still called the family's baby. Babyhood automatically ends for most children at the birth of the next sibling, or in a close extended family, at the birth of a cousin. Mothers date events in the past with "Mary or Johnny was my baby then."

Although local health authorities actively encourage breast-feeding, none of the mothers interviewed did so. Nursing is not a community practice. The reason given by the mothers for bottle feeding is increased freedom for them. Infants begin eating solids—highly seasoned beans and rice—at about three months. The bottle feeding seems to last as long as the child demands it. For the children studied here, the girls stopped bottle feeding between one and two, but the boys continued until three and in two cases, until age five. After bottle feeding is discontinued, milk is rarely served to children.

From birth to about three months, the child sleeps in a small basket or crib, usually in the parents' room or with other family members. Outgrowing this sleeping accommodation the baby moves into one of the double beds with the mother (if no male is present) or with the other children. Baby beds are seldom needed.

Childhood   "Children" are in a separate category from babies. They are seldom held or caressed. In fact, in contrast to babies they appear to be treated rather harshly. They can be screamed at or struck at will. As "children," they have responsibilities: watching another child, going to the store, or helping to clean the house. Needless to say, these activities do not begin immediately at the yard walking stage (eighteen to twenty-four months) but are fully recognized by adults and children by age four. A four-year-old handles money, household tasks, and increasing independence. By this age autonomy outside the house is virtually complete. The children roam at will through the neighborhood, never wandering beyond Rosepoint.

All the mothers interviewed expressed the firm desire not to have any more children. This is evidenced by a wide participation in the Louisiana Family Planning Program Clinic in New Orleans and an interest in birth control. However, these same mothers with large families are frequently scheming to get access to babies. Unwed girls expecting a baby are besieged with offers from family members. There appears to be something very desirable about enjoying a child part time or temporarily without having ultimate responsibility or the pains of pregnancy and childbirth.

Many households have extra children. In addition to the trades already accomplished, the feasibility of more "rematches" is constantly under discussion. Two of the families have in the past tried out a nephew, found the arrangement unsatisfactory, and sent the child back. One child, even two, more or less, inconveniences no one. The attitudes of the mothers can be summed up in this way: "I love having babies, they are wonderful to have around; it's the children that get on your nerves." Babies do not have the potential to act as "bad" as children do.

Childhood, from yard walking to first grade, offers no other major changes. However, first grade is a significant dividing line. This period lasts until school is finished or early adulthood reached, whichever comes first. When children start school, parental attitudes change considerably. Now for the first time, the parent and child may have long conversations. Parents may teach them games, usually card games, and the child is expected to observe certain social responsibilities like manners, for example.

The break from home-bound five-year olds to school-bound six-year olds is marked by the sporadic imposition of bedtime rules. These rules are as often broken as observed, but the verbal rationalization exists that now these children need their sleep. At school age the child also acquires a wardrobe, as befits his more public role.

Given the age at which boys drop out of school and girls assume mature sexual roles, adolescence is vastly attenuated and young adulthood begins by age fourteen for some. The outward symbols of this inward change are educational termination, increased sexual activities, and, for the girls, a change in hair styles. The laboriously achieved, ever-present braids of little girls are exchanged for the straight hair of womanhood.

Of the nine women questioned in this regard all readily volunteered the information that they had been engaged in an active sex life since age fourteen. One married at this age and had five children by age twenty; four others had children within two years, while the others did not settle down to a family life until about seventeen.

During these adolescent years the mothers and daughters become close friends, especially if the daughter has begun assuming the adult prerogatives of child-bearing. It must be remembered that many Rosepoint grandmothers are only thirty years old and not yet beyond their own period of fertility. This telescoping of generations is an important feature of the social structure.

It is not infrequent that the husband and father of the family will go away to live with another woman, become her common-law husband, and help raise *her* children. The fathers of the women in families one, two, and four have all become second fathers in families other than the one they sired. For the males, adolescence is a carefree period of sitting on the levee, partying, having affairs for which no consequences are demanded, and finally, the army, a job, or marriage. In community mores these are approved activities.

In the case of one family the wife remembers the years from thirteen to eighteen as the golden days of youth. She went to bars every night, flirted or slept with those she fancied, and spent the money from her job as a restaurant cook on clothes and luxuries. When at eighteen she became pregnant, her mother was delighted and was very much opposed to her marrying anyone. The mother envisioned her daughter remaining at home cooking, cleaning, and washing while she, the grandmother, raised the child. However, the daughter was determined to marry: "She know whose door to be knocking on." Five months pregnant and wearing a blue handkerchief on a white dress, she married. As a consolation prize, the grandmother was to raise the baby. Unfortunately, he died, but the grandmother had rights to the next one and is now raising him. Today, with five children of their own, they are, in terms of this community, a model of familial bliss, raising yet another generation.

"THEM CHILDREN"—VALUES IN CHILD REARING

What a mother *reports* to a social scientist that she would say or do to an unruly child may be less important to his language development than her frequently unarticulated and unexamined premises on the nature of children and her role in their growth. The unspoken philosophies about child-rearing techniques in a family or community are directly related to the kinds of language chosen.

As an example of this within one American subculture, the study of a predominantly middle-class New England town reveals the parents' preoccupation with their children *as potential*. What they will do or be when they grow up is a category of events to be speculated on and talked about.

> The infant as a potential is thought to be a bundle of largely inherited latent traits of emotional expression and abilities for achieving goals, which can only be realized gradually as the child develops and which may be influenced by training and growth. Most of the goals available to the children and adults of this community are thought to call for particular skills and a particular personality type, both of which must develop naturally or be influenced to develop out of the latent traits in the infant's potential . . . Divining for the potential is highly developed in the community. There are, of course, the formal tests for intelligence, personality and achievement, but there are also more subtle techniques, such as informal questioning of the child or observing his behavior for clues (Fischer and Fischer 1966: 50–51).

In contrast, many discussions in Rosepoint about children begin and end with the phrase, "Them children, they so bad." This statement may be heard many times a day and is the almost certain answer to any questions about children. Probes as to the reasons for "bad children" receive a more firmly reiterated "Them children, they so bad." Every member of the community readily agrees, "You right about that." There is no need to discuss why they are bad; it is a fact that they are. Rationales elicited by persistent probing are *non sequiturs* or are references to the child's immediate actions. Their philosophy can be seen in the following incidents.

One father of eight, four by his first marriage and four by the previous marriages of his present wife, said that they were bad because he "ain't had time to love all them children." He was at that time affectionately cuddling his second wife's nieces as well as his own stepdaughters.

In the kitchen of one family, the mother commented several times on how *bad* her two children were and how she does not want any more. When pressed on what constitutes "badness," she did not answer. Later the two-year-old son pulled off his shoes and was sitting at the table quietly blowing bubbles into his bottle of coke with a straw. She pointed to him and said, "See how bad they is." Throughout the day he had been amusing himself. He sat in his mother's lap or wrestled with his sister, seldom speaking.

In another family the mother volunteers this information to the investigator.

MOTHER: Romulus is so bad. [*He is four.*]
INVESTIGATOR: Why do you say that?
MOTHER: That child, *he so bad.* [*Afterthought*] I be whip him every day every
        day. [*Calls to child in next room*] Romulus, hear, I'm ona whip you.
ROMULUS: [*Calmly and casually*] I'm ona whip you.

The mother laughs. She considers the episode ended. Anyone who could not tell that her children were bad would not profit from explanations.

One woman commented that her brother, whom she has raised, was bad. When asked why and how he was bad, she repeated, as though it could be only too obvious, "he just be *bad*." Pressured as to how one could know this, she said to look at his smile: "it sneaky."

Speaking is often equated with the quality "bad." A twelve-month baby sat absolutely still on the couch for an hour. His mother commented that her baby was "good": he could not yet talk. When babies learn to talk they are "bad children."

The second most frequent statement of the mothers is "Them children worry my nerve." Not infrequently this is the reason given for bad children. Why are they bad? They work on your nerves. These are the only statements ever volunteered to explain a given child-rearing practice. Other statements or rationales can be elicited but may never occur in the absence of a curious investigator.

The statement, "Them children worry my nerve," is the prototype for elaborations:

"Them children so doggone slow."
"Them children run me crazy."
"Them children, they horrible."

Explanations about individual children are only variations of the theme:

"That child, he horrible."
"That child, she something else."

In one interview a mother and grandmother many times answered each question about children with the above set beginning "them children" and all questions about specific children with "That child, she something else."

The vagueness of these answers is significant. "My children" collectively are seldom discussed. "I brung my children to New Orleans" (all her children and no one else's). "I thank God, all my children born healthy" (those to whom she gave birth). Her socialization philosophy centers on children as a category and not just her very own children. "Them children," as the basis of her outlook, refers to all one's own children, plus those one may be raising part time, and all others within sight or sound. Caretaking duties belong to any relative or friend, young or old, who is near the child. No mother is threatened when other adults in the community discipline her children. In fact, they are invited to do so.

Discipline here means the entire area of personal and social control—a major part of the mother's role. Discipline is uniform: what applies to one child applies to another. Events subject to disciplinary action are not anticipatory; that is, children are controlled as the need arises. No one draws upon collective experience to imagine dangers or problems which affect their children. Children are not warned, admonished, or hit with rules unless the specific need for such has already risen. Thus no child will be warned as he leaves the house not to trespass the boundaries, unless he has done so before and been punished for it. This control and its verbal correlates will be discussed more fully in chapter six.

The general philosophy for coping with standard socialization problems is not to worry about them. Problems familiar to Dr. Spock fans like thumb sucking, bedwetting, eating ashes or dirt, beating animals, playing with knives, or sleeping and eating irregularities are in one definition of reality serious aspects of physical and mental health. But in local definition children grow up or they die. There is, therefore, no correspondingly well-developed philosophy to resolve such annoyances. If attitudes toward a child's physical health are casual, then attitudes about his cognitive and psychological development are more so. Keeping her children well-fed is regarded as the mother's major task.

The entire socialization process is characterized by a lack of piousness and sentimentality about children. The following will illustrate. A two-year-old boy had been crying all day and wanted to be held. "Poor baby," commented a visitor, to which the mother replied: "Poor baby!! You mean 'Poor mother.'" Another mother, warned that her two-year-old was about to catch his fingers in the car door, replied, "Good, teach him a lesson." Children are not delicate or sensitive. *Nothing* is censored for their ears. Except for Saturday-night parties, they may go anywhere. Explanations such as "I'll have more time with my children," "Small children must not be left alone," are too sentimental. The pop psychology of women's magazines and bestselling books on child-rearing is not read or quoted. There are no fads in raising children. There is instead, "That's the way they brung us up."

The attitudes about child-rearing in Rosepoint can be contrasted with those of ostensibly sophisticated middle-class parents under the spell of Freudian psychology. To an observer it seems that such parents believe in a kind of witchcraft: something which they do may inadvertently cripple their child psychologically; some rite or ritual performed incorrectly, or the "wrong" attitude toward feeding and bodily function warps potential. One popular book (Ginott 1965) offers parents the appropriate verbal responses (incantations?) for the crises of childhood. Failure to observe the magical prescriptions results in faulty parent–child relationships. Yet, at a time when middle-class parents worry about the resolution of Oedipal conflicts in their children and in themselves, many of Rosepoint's children grow up without fathers, living alternately in the homes of aunts, sisters, or grandmothers. They are provided with "love" which is defined as sufficient food, housing, and affection. No one worries about "psychosocial development," "creativity," "adjustment," or potential. Parents do not hex or bewitch their children into neuroses in Rosepoint.

4 / A Rosepoint child: the boundary of experiences

NATALIE: What you all go play outside?
ANNE: Ball.
NATALIE: What kind of ball?
ANNE: Basketball.
NATALIE: Basketball and what else?
ANNE: This.
NATALIE: Yeah, what is this? What is that?
ANNE: Ball.
NATALIE: A ball eh.
ANNE: Yeah.
NATALIE: I see. And what you all was coming over here tell Fortrel what was on that track? (*sic*) What does stop on that track out there? Hunh, what does stop on that track out there, Anne? Anne, what does stop on that track outside? Anne?
ANNE: I don't know.
LIZ: You didn't see—
NATALIE: [*Interrupting*] Listen, what stop on that track?
ANNE: Hunh?
NATALIE: What that stop on that track?
ANNE: I don't know.
FORTREL: A train.
NATALIE: A what?
FORTREL: [*More firmly*] A train.
NATALIE: That's right.
LIZ: He talk when he want. He just don't want.
FORTREL: A train! A train!!
NATALIE: Yeah, a train.

NATALIE: [*Laughing*] And where we going this evening?
FORTREL: Hunh?
NATALIE: Where we going this evening?
FORTREL: To the ball.
NATALIE: No! Where I'm gonna take you this evening?
FORTREL: Hunh?
NATALIE: Now sit down!! Where I'm gonna take you all this evening?
FORTREL: To Champagne. [*A store down the road*]
NATALIE: Hunh?
FORTREL: To Champagne.
NATALIE: To Champagne. NO.

The bulk of the fieldwork for this study was devoted to accompanying and observing families in their routine activities. A daily diary was obtained for the preschool children of each family by following a child through his ordinary activities and observing his range of movement, and interactions with other children and adults. Mothers were interviewed as to children's activities at times not directly observable by the fieldworker. Knowledge of these patterns yields an idea of the total range of the child's experience and exposure. In a general sense, the range of experiential limits is a map of the conceptual limits. Scores on verbal ability tests, for example, correlate with the socioeconomic or ethnic background of children (Bernstein 1962, 1964; Anastasi and de Jesus 1953). Presumably, the child's experiences in a different social and linguistic environment create communication patterns specific to a subculture.

Also sought is information about the child's linguistic contacts: to whom does he talk, who talks to him, what do they talk about, under what circumstances does he use language or need to respond. In other words, what is his *language diet*? Such data are important as they reveal the range or potential of linguistic opportunities. What a child is exposed to as primary sensory data may affect his vocabulary as well as the type of topics he can discuss.

Rosepoint regards itself as a community and the people feel an identity with each other. From an outsider's point of view they are characterized by more prolonged and frequent interaction with each other than with any other group. Because of this, Rosepoint is a speech community (for other examples, see Gumperz 1964). This means that Rosepoint is the primary reference group for the child's language development. To what extent will the child ever be exposed to other speech communities? Will he regularly move outside this circle of relatives and friends who share a common culture? What kind of language different from that of his own speech community could he expect to hear? For the best description of the philosophy and theory underlying these approaches and concerns, see Dell Hymes (1961, 1962).

THE DAILY ROUTINE

From field notes and interviews, a typical day in the life of a Rosepoint child is reconstructed. The day appears to be the same for any child eighteen months to first grade. Children younger than that do not play outside.

5:00 to 6:00 A.M. The family gets up. The mother fixes breakfast and the father leaves for work. The school-age children are up. The preschool children may stay in bed longer since they stayed up later.

6:00 to 8:00 A.M. They bathe, several children to a tub of water. Families without running water bathe at relatives' houses or in tubs at convenient times. All dress and make beds, children assisting. Then children gather up their soiled clothes and towels, putting them near the washing machine. Older children leave for school. The TV cartoons are on. Soon it is time for rerun situation comedies and the morning quiz and game shows. The TV usually remains on throughout the day.

8:00 to 10:00 A.M. The mother puts clothes in the machine. She sends a child to the store for soap powder, rice, or cokes and gives him an extra nickel to spend for candy. On the way he collects other children and shares some candy with them. Usually he sees other adults who ask him what his mother is doing and who may give him a message to deliver to her. The beans are put on to cook and the dishes are stacked in the sink. Either the mother sweeps with a broom or she tells an older child to do it. She is frequently interrupted by the telephone, if there is one, occasional demands by the child, vendors in the street, or visitors at the door.

10:00 A.M. to 12:00 noon Time for marketing. If the family does not own a car, the mother sends a child to a relative's house to tell them to "bring her to the market." On the way she stops at the post office for money orders and at the Public Service office to pay bills. The children know this routine by heart. Automatically they climb into the car. No information or questions are exchanged. At the bank suckers are passed out. The children wait unattended in the car while their mother is conducting business. However, at the market everyone goes in to check out the toy and candy counter. The clerks recognize local kids but do not speak to them. They may quietly ask for and receive some kind of small treat. Sometimes the mother is in a hurry. At home the mother puts a little meat on to cook.

12:00 noon to 3:00 P.M. The day's food is cooked. Portions will be taken from a large pot on the stove throughout the day, until it is finished late at night. The children may eat at any time for the rest of the day if they feel hungry. They will probably not eat when their parents do. When they indicate readiness to eat, the mother serves the food and mixes it all together in a bowl. Nothing else but the food in the bowl is eaten. Only spoons are used. After the meal is finished the children receive some Koolaid or soft drink. Young boys are sometimes given a bottle with milk in it. Otherwise, milk is rare. None of the children takes official naps, that is, naps ordained and supervised by the mother. At the age of physical mobility, children fall asleep, when and if they desire, any place they happen to be. This is continued through adolescence and into adulthood unless school or work interferes. Children from infancy on have the complete choice to nap or not.

Meanwhile, the mother is listening to television serials, doing odd jobs such as hanging out clothes and cleaning the kitchen, or visiting with friends. The children play both outside and inside alternately. They prefer to be inside if anything is happening. But the mother orders them outside if she is bothered by them. During this period, if the day's work is done or if she feels like it, they go visiting. Some of the children may already be visiting a grandmother or aunt, but those in evidence accompany her. During the visit the children either play outside with the children of the host or sit quietly and listen to the adults talk.

3:00 to 5:00 P.M. The older children come home from school at 3:00. They change their clothes and do their chores and homework, eating when they feel like it. The mother is finishing up any chores and shopping left to be done or watching the serials on television with the children. Most of the children play outside as they wait for the school children and the working men to return.

In the lane.

5:00 P.M. to bedtime This is the most relaxed time of the day. The mother's daily tasks are finished. Anything else she does is optional. Everyone eats and goes to bed at his pleasure. The television is always on and the entire family watches. The father bathes, eats, and may sit on the levee with his friends while it is still light. Adults and teenage family members might attend meetings, choir practice, ball games, or frequent the local bars.

This schedule may not actually reveal the flexibility and genuine lack of set times for doing set things. There is no such time as "lunch time," "dinner time," "naptime," or "bedtime." These events occur as the individual spirit moves. Certain tasks in particular must be done and cannot be avoided: cooking (a lengthy process without convenience foods), laundry (an even lengthier process without drier or wringer), and minimal household maintenance. Children in particular construct their own schedules. The basics of life—eating, sleeping, playing outside, television, and visiting—are not rigidly blocked off for them into named time periods.

This perfunctory schedule does not reveal another significant feature of a child's life: the high frequency with which he spends the day at the home of some friend or relative. The day's activities remain unchanged. The house, the food, the noises, and the smells are similar. Only the personnel will be different.

In the same manner, an additional child or children stay at his house. Cousins trade off at will. It is a rare day when the "sleep-in" occupants are the only ones to eat out of the common kettle. The continual influx of visitors of all ages provides the surest break in the day's routine. The knowledge that hungry friends and relatives will drop by to check out the pot is a predictable element in the daily schedule.

WEEKLY, MONTHLY, AND YEARLY ROUTINES

Sunday as a day has a special character. Relatives living in the New Orleans area return to the home fold. Everyone is dressed up, even children who have only one or two weekday outfits. In most large households, however, the cooking, laundering, and cleaning must still be done. Church services and eating are the main events. The Sunday feasting includes filé gumbo, baked macaroni, potato salad, peas, corn, rice dressing, stewed chicken or crayfish bisque in season. Not the usual weekday beans!

None of the churches provide Sunday Schools for the children. Attendance at services is sporadic and not expected from preschoolers. There is no institutionalized means for their participation in community religious life until they are older. The only other activities during the week for children are a rare school function or shopping trip to a nearby town. If anything special is to occur, Sunday is the day.

The traditional American holidays are celebrated: Halloween, Easter, Thanksgiving, and the Fourth of July. Local Catholic holidays, All Saints' Day, and Mardi Gras are observed by a church service and the gathering of the relatives for feasting and drinking. Once a year comes the opportunity to witness the spectacular parades of the Carnival season. While these holidays are a momentary break in the year's calendar, as a celebration they are merely an extension of the regular Sunday fare. The Christmas and summer vactions provide the two most exciting peaks in the yearly cycle. Because birthdays and Saint's days are not commemorated by gift giving, Christmas is the only occasion when presents are purchased for children.

Summer vacations are spent in New Orleans at the homes of relatives, a visit later reciprocated. A special outing may be planned: the zoo, a movie, the "Burger King," a Canal Street shopping trip or a family wedding or christening. These, however, are rare events and may not occur more than twice a year during childhood.

None of the children in these households has ever been to Baton Rouge or further than seventy miles from home in any direction. Some of the adults have been to California or Chicago, where they have relatives. For long journeys trains are virtually the only form of travel and the only reason for such an arduous trip is to visit the relatives on the other end. Sight-seeing as such is unheard of.

NON-KIN ENCOUNTERS FOR CHILDREN

Passing through the lives of these children daily are a succession of "resource" people not related to them. By "resource" is meant the human contacts available for linguistic exploitation. Who these people are as a category, how the children react to them, and how they are trained to react yields another view of their environment. As in many rural communities throughout America, busy and supposedly home-bound housewives are visited routinely by tradesmen. In Rosepoint, where all lanes are parallel to each other and the only connecting perpendicular is the River Road, the tradesman's car or truck passes down the lane honking to notify the inhabitants that he will stop when the lane ends and he turns around. Usually no such signal is necessary since the community possesses a "distant early warning system," the children. Even in the house with the telelvision on, they know which tradesman is coming down the lane. If they have been playing in the yard, they will know which salesmen are on adjacent lanes and the time interval before reaching them. Moreover, they will remember all who have passed that day in case the mother has been absent. The children know the car, the sound of the horn, the mission and schedule of these tradesmen and probably respond as well to other cues lost to adults.

The following is a list of these tradesmen:

1. Daily: baker, butcher
2. Weekly or twice weekly:
   Insurance (health, life or property)
   Cleaners (there are no public cleaners, only the house-to-house collectors)
   Salesman for 45 R.P.M. records (Saturday afternoon after payday)
   Fishman on Fridays
   Vegetable seller in season
   Avon lady, or door-to-door cosmetic salesman
3. Monthly: the dry goods salesman; the parish bookmobile; those selling "chances" for the local churches

This means an average of three commercial visits per day.

The children not only serve as memory-storage banks but as messengers. They frequently deliver simple instructions from their mother to the tradesmen: "stop by here on your way back," "three bags of donuts," "some shallots," "my mama say she pay you next week." Apart from delivering instructions and making requests for goods and services, the children never speak to these tradesmen. If children have not initiated a conversation in this way, the tradesmen will not talk to them. In contrast to the shy children, the adults often conduct lengthy conversations with salesmen.

The same pattern is evident when children enter community stores to spend their own nickel or that of their friends, or to run an errand for their mother. Since few in the area can afford to shop weekly, the daily trips to the store for the essentials of the moment are a major part of the routine. Children over the age of three can walk to the small food stores within Rosepoint, but they drive with their parents or relatives to the stores in Vacherie. Within these mercantile contacts, no one speaks to the children and the children do not speak unless they must deliver a message or need assistance.[1]

To summarize: children do not and are not expected to speak to tradesmen, merchants, and other functionaries either in public or at home, unless there is an evident reason. They are spared the necessity of answering since few if any of

---

[1] See Roger G. Barker and Herbert Wright, *Midwest and Its Children*, (1954), for a discussion of the importance of commercial contacts in child development.

these visitors speak to them. It is possible that this pattern is a part of black-white relations in the South. That certain speaking patterns are reserved for these encounters is well known. However, not all the tradesmen and merchants are white, and the pattern prevails regardless of color. The same rule also seems to apply when visiting with black friends outside the community. Grownups find stores a part of an effective grapevine, and when in stores they talk insatiably. The children are silent and reserved.

The last major category of non-kin encounters is with family friends or distant, seldom seen relatives. Here again, away from the familiar surroundings, the child seems to know what is expected—silence. At any age a child visiting someone not seen daily will remain very quiet, perhaps observing and listening. At the first disturbance, he will be sent outside immediately with no attempt to disguise the reason for the parent's displeasure. "Wouldn't you like to play with so-and-so," attempts to mollify him with food and toys, or supposedly subtle references to the consequences of incurring parental wrath are strategies not employed. The choice is clear and immediate: be inconspicuous or be absent. This injunction applies to toddlers and older children. Infants and crawlers who can not be placed in the temporary care of an older child will be ignored, fed, or held, but not spoken to. This does not mean ostracism for them but merely that it is more desirable to talk to adults.

It seems possible from this evidence that children are not expected to interact verbally in non-kin encounters. Children should be seen and not heard. Within the extended circle of relatives and very close friends, however, this stricture on speech is broken. The silent absorption in community life, the participation in the daily commercial rituals, and the hours spent apparently overhearing adults' conversations should not be underestimated in their impact on a child's language growth.

PHYSICAL ENVIRONMENT

In addition to the yard in which every child plays, there are sugar cane fields adjoining the lots. Before the fall harvest, the sweet round sticks are an endless source of amusement. The other fields either lie fallow or provide pasture for the cattle. The paths across the fields, the junk thrown in them, and the pecan groves are playgrounds for all children. No yards are fenced and all contain open sewers in which to play. The lack of sidewalks, closed sewers, curbs, paved roads, or inside storage facilities creates a feeling of dirt and clutter. However, the yard with its clothespins, bottles, pigpen, various tubs and cans, old cars, sticks, tools, automobile parts, and running sewer water, is a child's richest playground.

The insides of many homes are quite dark. Some have only shutters instead of glass windows. All are poorly lighted. Catalogues, the *Louisiana Weekly* (a black newspaper), or an occasional TV Guide constitute the only reading matter in evidence.

The level of noise in these homes is extremely high. Either the radio, television, or record player is playing loudly, competing with the washing machine and the

A four-year-old amuses himself in the yard.

sounds of daily life in a large family. It is the parents' custom, regardless of the message, to shout. The verbal, vocal, and mechanical noise level is generally very high. By contrast, the children seem very silent.

TOYS AS PART OF LEARNING ENVIRONMENT

Toys and the attitudes surrounding their place in growth are of crucial importance in intellectual development, if only from the viewpoint that the curriculum of the primary grades revolves around the manipulation of objects. In a recent article, Bernstein and Young (1968) found significant differences between middle- and working-class families in regard to their conceptions of the learning potentials of toys. Many of the middle-class mothers felt that toys helped the child to explore his environment, that is, "find out about things" (1968:132), and were not merely a way to keep their children occupied. A high correlation was obtained between mothers who thought this and those whose children scored well on intelligence tests.

> Thus for the working-class child a whole order of potential learning may not be available. By similar argument, it can be said that inasmuch as the middle-class mother's concept of the use of toys is in harmony with that of the Infant School, then the middle-class child is more likely than the working-class child to explore profitably the potentiality of the infant class . . . The working-class child

may have to learn what for the middle-class child is given by his primary social-ization. It would seem that, even at the age of five years, there is differential access to processes which facilitate the development of the ability and the oppor-tunity to benefit from school (Bernstein and Young 1968:138).

A survey concerned not about opinions on but about the actual incidence of toys was conducted among the seven families in this study. A list was made of all the toys played with by children. In some homes toys that had been stored (for no apparent reason) were kindly shown to the investigator. Such a survey was made possible by the limited number of toys available and by the intimate nature of the project.

What types of toys are to be found in these homes? The most ubiquitous cate-gory is wheeled vehicles: strollers, walkers, tricycles, and bicycles. Each of these is an age-graded toy. No one child has exclusive possession unless he is the only child of that size. Instead, the vehicle is used jointly by all the children of the appropriate age within the family. The luckiest children of all have access to an abandoned car. Unfortunately, many of the bikes and trikes become broken, are never fixed, and remain inoperative. Having access to wheeled transportation, even for small babies, is a major value in this culture.

In addition, all the homes have catalogues for light reading and a wide range of small objects for sucking. The latter include aspirin bottles, inexpensive plastic toys, and baby bottles. Boys in particular are seldom without something to chew on.

"On the road." The school is in the background.

All homes have some kind of mock household implements for the little girls. Though intended for girls, the boys enjoy them too. Ironing boards, irons, stoves with a little light to cook with, and make-believe washing machines are items distributed at least one to a home. These items can hardly be called make-believe in view of the ever-present realities of cooking, ironing, and washing and the early age at which a female will assume some responsibilities for these tasks. As child care falls among these harsher realities, it is surprising that dolls are quite infrequent. Dolls with movable parts, expensively dressed, and usually dark-skinned are carefully stored. Small girls do not carry dolls around, or feed, diaper, and love them; some girls have, in fact, never had a doll of their own. Of course they have almost unlimited access to the real thing.

Other types of toys appear only occasionally: balls, toy guns, plastic objects, color books, balloons, jacks, and the sort of twenty-five cent to fifty cent novelties bought off revolving racks in drugstores. One family had a View-Master but had purchased no slides to accompany it and had to use newspaper instead—an unsatisfactory substitute. Still, it was suitable to chew on. Another family spent the children's Christmas budget on football uniforms for all the boys. Footballs, baseballs, and inflated rubber balls are shared by all the children of the family and the neighbors' families. With strenuous play the balls become useless and are discarded. Thus ball playing is almost a cyclical sport. All ages of children play with balls if they are available.

Occupying the major portion of the children's time are articles and opportunities of all kinds found in the yard. Water tubs, old spoons, sugar cane in season, pot handles, broken bottles, and hundreds of other objects are endless sources of entertainment. If toys and play allow chances to manipulate and explore the environment, then these children take full advantage. However, as Bernstein and Young (1969:138) point out, this is not a type of environment which in any way resembles the public schools which the children must enter.

The significance of the differential between the preschool environment and the school is emphasized by the absence of the types of toys favored by schools. There are no books written especially for children, nor are there so-called educational toys designed to teach colors, shapes, spatial relationships, textures, or elementary mechanics. There are no paints, or finger painting, no clay, only crayons infrequently. The child's first exposure to exercise equipment—swings, slides, climbers, and teeter-totters—will come when he enters the first grade.

One of the reasons for this configuration of toys is the lack of money. What little cash is available is used to satisfy the expressed wants of the child. As considerable financial sacrifices are made, parents cannot afford to buy what the child says he wants as well as the other toys which might serve an educational purpose.

TRAVELING: THE "CHARITY-CANAL" COMPLEX

Parts of New Orleans are, in the eyes of country folk, just an extension of Vacherie. For the children, these urban areas comprise a limited, familiar experience. Charity Hospital is probably the most important institution, *per se*, in the lives of people whose low income qualifies them for admittance. Seldom a week goes by that friends or relatives do not make the long drive or bus ride to attend the Out-Patient Clinic, have a baby or a prenatal check, visit relatives, or take turns sitting with a sick child. Those who by dint of limited social mobility no longer qualify for hospital services still go to visit the ill or take advantage of emergency treatment. Pregnant women whose labor pains are five to ten minutes apart will secure a ride to New Orleans, breaking the speed limits in hopes of attracting the attention of a policeman to give them an all-sirens escort to Charity. Although a confusing assortment of local doctors and tiny hospitals are available to paying patients in the Vacherie area, local medical facilities do not enjoy the prestige and confidence of Charity.

The bus for New Orleans leaves Vacherie about 6:00 A.M. and arrives at Krauss Department Store on Canal Street about 8:00 A.M. Later, in the afternoon, the bus departs from the same place. After the visiting hours at Charity or a long wait in the Out-Patient Clinics, there are hours left to be occupied before returning on the bus. So the visitors "walk the street," the only street that matters, which is Canal. Here the discount houses, bargain shops, and dime stores offer shoes, clothes, and household goods with seemingly low prices, wide choices, and all the glamor of a Canal Street purchase. Most of the really important purchases are made on Canal, due in part to the magic and in part to the relative lack of consumer goods, particularly clothes, in Vacherie.

The street which connects Charity Hospital on Tulane Avenue with Canal Street is South Rampart, long the unofficial center of black culture in New Orleans. There are other perpendicular streets but only Rampart matters in the minds of these visitors. Lining this particular segment of Rampart are pawn and hock shops, one appropriately called the "Eagle Loan Shop." This route, Tulane Avenue to Rampart to Canal Street and back, is New Orleans to many black countrymen. Other ways of spending a carefree day in the city are not utilized. None of these informants had been to the French Quarter, the Public Library, or Audubon Park.

OTHER TRAVELS: "ON THE ROAD"

If the Charity-Canal complex is the public side of New Orleans, there is also the private side: the close relatives who now live in the city. These rural–urban migrants tend to settle together. Most Rosepoint people have relatives in Harvey, Gretna, or Marrero (small cities on the west bank across from New Orleans). This is probably due as much to the tendency to settle where one already has contacts as to the fact that these people seek employment at nearby Avondale Shipping Yards. There is frequent visiting back and forth and trading vacations at each other's homes. These relatives provide the only other contact with urban life available to Rosepoint dwellers.

Traveling within the more familiar Vacherie area is different. The roads of rural Louisiana parishes have sidewalks along one edge. Even cane fields have sidewalks, some fully paved. Wherever there is a road there is a walk, if only a trail. The importance of this for an area without local public transportation and a median annual income of $1872 is clear.[2] Walking, however necessary, has a distinctly unpleasant connotation and is to be avoided at all costs. Only self-admitted eccentrics walk anywhere. Somewhere, somehow, in the network of friends and relatives a car must be located, even if the trip is only a block. Children walk everywhere rather than stay at home, but the greatest joy of their lives is a car ride. Those adults who have cars use them extensively at the request of others. Sharing wheeled transportation is an integral part of community life.

Clearly enunciated principles of travel exist and are seldom violated. The first of these is that if one is in a hurry it is all right to travel alone within but never outside Vacherie. Since there are fewer cars than eager-to-travel adults, it is easy to find a companion. Traveling is not a solitary endeavor. Children figure as incidentals in all this traveling: like the poor, "they are always with us." The second rule is to avoid if possible going anywhere unfamiliar unless several experienced adult friends are along. This apprehension about new places and new people is partially correlated with the requirements for survival known to blacks in the South. What once may have had survival value is now a cultural habit. For example, many of the people in Rosepoint go to an optometrist on Canal Street (if they go at all) because he is known to them, not because he is close, reasonably priced, or well trained.

Few can read a road map. Instead the community and family provide a "cognitive map," just as real, which consists of where they have been before, where they have friends and relatives, and where they are known and well-treated. Everyone in the community has been to most of the same places, and the children will go only where the adults are accustomed to going. There are few travel experiences to be shared vicariously.

---

[2] This figure is taken from the 1960 Census and applies to the non-white population of the Parish. However, even if this sum has doubled in the decade since, cars are still a luxury. U.S. Department of Commerce, Bureau of the Census, *United States Census of Population: 1960*, Vol. I, *Characteristics of the Population*, part 20, Louisiana, Table 88, page 225.

5 / "Teaching" them children to talk

I

KATHY: Go store Mommy.
    MOTHER: Oh, you want to go to the store?
    KATHY: Go now.
    MOTHER: We can't go now. We have to eat dinner.
KATHY: Eat dinner.

II

    MOTHER: Sing something what Jame Brown just sing.
        What Jame Brown just sing?
        What James Brown just sing, Forry?
    CHILD: [*Sings*]
    MOTHER: What else Jame Brown sing? What else he sing? What he sing?
    CHILD: Jame Brown say "I'm black and proud."
    MOTHER: What he say?
    FORTREL: Black and proud! Black and proud!
    MOTHER: Jame Brown say what?
    CHILD: Black and proud!
    MOTHER: And what else he say?

The first tape (recorded by the author) was taken from a white middle-class family; the second from a Rosepoint family. As we shall see from similar conversations, there are differences in the manner in which the Rosepoint mothers and middle-class mothers perceive their role as "teacher." Sometimes this interpretation has subtle linguistic consequences. Children of both types of families acquire language and the ability to communicate within their own communities; but the pattern of their socialization is distinct. This chapter will survey instruction in the mechanics of language itself, instruction in the social context for using language, and the unconscious learning about basic postulates of the culture which result from different forms of instruction.

EXPANSIONS

It has been postulated by some observers that a child approximates well-formed syntax by repeating an utterance or partial utterance of an adult or in turn having his telegraphic speech expanded into an acceptable sentence.

There is one respect in which parental speech is not random. Quite often adults repeat the speech of small children and, in so doing, change the children's sentences into the nearest well-formed adult equivalent. Brown has called this phenomenon "expansion of child speech" (Brown 1964). It is a kind of imitation in reverse, in which the parent echoes the child and, at the same time, supplies features that are missing from the child's sentence (McNeill 1966:73).

These expansions were given much attention because they appeared so frequently in the speech of the adults and children studied by Brown and Bellugi (1964); Miller and Ervin (1964); and Braine (1963).

The mothers of Adam and Eve responded to the speech of their children with expansions about 30 percent of the time . . . A reduced or incomplete English sentence seems to constrain the English-speaking adult to expand it into the nearest properly formed complete sentence (Brown and Bellugi 1964:144).

A middle-class American adult is seldom able to resist turning "Daddy bye-bye" into "Daddy's gone bye-bye." Frequently, a declarative intonation serves to validate the child's observation, while a rising, "Daddy's gone bye-bye?" serves as a communication check.

Typical child sentences and their expansions follow:

This ring.	This is a round ring.
Donnie all-gone.	Is Donnie all-gone?
It a bus.	Is it a bus?

(Ervin 1966:168)

No native speaker of English could confuse the mother's expansions with the baby's sentences. Not surprisingly, whole grammars of these utterances have been written in an attempt to equate the expansions with linguistic input and output.

If parental expansion of child speech contributed significantly to adult norms of grammar, the situation of the children of Rosepoint would be lamentable. In less than five per cent of the total utterances recorded were reciprocal expansions clearly operative in either child's or parents' speech. The mothers occasionally enhance the pivot structures of the younger children, but not with the same frequency as would a middle-class adult. Three, four, and five morpheme sentences from older children were repeated or expanded with even less frequency. To illustrate: the middle-class mothers of Adam and Eve (Brown's subject-children) would find it difficult, if not impossible, to spend an entire day with two, three, and four year olds without expanding or repeating a single utterance of the children. To do so is a part of their native speaker's intuition.

The mothers in the present study spend entire days in this manner and suffer not at all from a thwarted instinct. That is not to say that once in a while they do not expand or repeat a child's utterance in the same way as do Adam's or Eve's mother, but rather that such responses occur infrequently and without any evident compulsion.

A closer look at Brown and Bellugi's *Adam* transcripts explains the difference. Below is reproduced a segment of Adam's first record. Adam is at this point twenty-seven months old.

ADAM	MOTHER
See truck, Mommy.	Did you see the truck?
See truck.	No, you didn't see it.
	There goes one.
No I see truck.	
	Yes, there goes one.
There go one.	
See a truck.	
See truck Mommy.	
See truck.	
Truck.	
Put truck, Mommy.	Put the truck where?
Put truck window.	I think that one's too large to go
	in the window.

(Brown and Bellugi 1966:135).

Now note their comments on this speech sample.

> The dialogue between mother and child does not read like a transcribed dialogue between two adults . . . The conversation is, in the first place, very much in the here and now. (Brown and Bellugi 1966:134.)

Whatever its shortcomings, this little recording is clearly a conversation and a dialogue, but one type specific to mother-child interaction in this subculture.

Compare with the following. The child here is thirty-six months old, eighth of eight children, and son of a factory worker.

KENNETH: Mama, look, a train.
MOTHER: Yeah, Kenneth, I see it.

The child's attempt at initiating this conversation is quite like Adam's method, yet the responses of the mothers differ radically.

MOTHER: You pissy.
KENNETH: [*He says nothing; he knows it.*]
MOTHER: You piss in your pant.
KENNETH: [*Smiles.*]
MOTHER: You shame you piss in your pant?
KENNETH: No.
MOTHER: You should be.

Kenneth's mother is remarking in a sweet and gentle way; it may be a turn off, but not a put down.

In the next dialogue, a tape recording of a mother and her twenty-eight-month-old son, she initiates the conversation, determines the subject matter and direction. The lack of verbal reciprocity would seem to negate this as a conversation. However, the mother is pleased with its communicative success. The conversation is typical of mother-child interaction in Rosepoint.

Mark is playing with the knob on the television:

> MOTHER: Say, Mark, quit it.
>   Say, Mark, quit it!
>   Say, Mark, quit it! !
> *[She remarks that children pretend to be deaf when they do not want to listen.]*
> MOTHER: Mark, oh Mark, come give your mother a kiss.
>   Mark, oh Mark, come give your mother a kiss.
>   Mark, oh Mark, come give mama a kiss.
> *[She gets no response at all.]*
> MOTHER: Oh, nobody to kiss me.
> *[She tries a new tact.]*
> MOTHER: Mark, take this belt to Cicero.
> *[After a long pause, Mark, attracted by her root beer, comes and sits on her lap. She shares her drink with him from the bottle.]*
> MOTHER: Mark, give me a kiss. He shame to kiss his mother in front of Joan. Mark, you shame to kiss your mama in front of Joan?[1] *[He still doesn't kiss her.]*

They watch a soap opera together. Later he tries to attract her attention by biting and kissing her.

The fundamental attitude of Kenneth's and Mark's mothers in these conversations is that *children do not function to uphold their end of the conversation.* Neither mother sees any point in training herself or her child to conduct a conversation on such minutiae as trucks and trains. As the taping sessions proved, the mothers were virtual strangers in talking to their children where talk for the sake of talk was required. She responds to questions and requests with as full a measure of love as does Adam's mother. She addresses him with the complete range of affects from rage to admiration, but she will not cater to his verbal whims. Small children learning to talk are not the sort of people with whom Rosepoint adults "engage in dialogue."

If a child has something important to say, his mother will listen, and he had better listen when she decides to tell him something. But for conversation, *per se,* for the sound of a human voice, she will go visiting, make phone calls, have company, or in sheer desperation talk to an older child (eight or above). She will never find herself politely trapped, as will Adam's mother, by the verbal precocity of a three year old, with whom one cannot honestly discuss an interesting issue.

Adam's mother is committed to talking with him often, an activity which involves expanding and imitating his speech as much as possible. This technique does not necessarily teach him language since children whose parents do not expand their utterances also learn to talk. With or without indirect instruction, the child learns that "no I see truck" becomes "I don't see the truck."

Just as Kenneth and Adam learn two different dialects of English, they also learn two different sociolinguistic dialects. The verbal tricks which Adam learns from his

---

[1] In the two previous conversations with Kenneth and Mark cited above, the mothers are using a form of appeal to the social oriented feeling of shame rather than to the personal oriented feelings of guilt. For more discussion of the implications of the guilt-shame complex in child-rearing, see Benedict (1946:222–223).

mother will stand him in better stead at middle-class schools than the verbal tricks Kenneth learns from his mother. Kenneth has not learned how to initiate and monopolize a conversation with an adult on a topic of his choosing. Mark has never been rewarded for verbal advances; no one expects him to say more than the bare minimum. Boys growing up in Rosepoint do not fill in the bare spaces of time with talk. No one in the community takes seriously the chattering of a child. In fact, as the conversations indicate, the children hold their parent's attention longer *if they say nothing.*

Kenneth and Mark have learned to amuse themselves, to sit very still and listen to adults talk, (timed at three hours on several occasions), and to play happily with siblings and other children for days on end. Their mothers do not exist for the amusement of children.

In an experiment to determine whether expansions of a child's speech would augment grammatical development, Cazden (1965) found that simply replying to what the child had said was just as effective in stimulating speech. Expansions are, it would seem, more helpful to certain groups of parents than to any group of children.

> A difference in the amount of parental expansion, in turn, might depend on the amount of interest parents have in understanding what their children say . . . We might expect that the tendency to expand is greatest among those parents with a conviction that children do have something to say, parents who believe that the behavior of children is worthy of attention, parents who are, in short, subscribers to middle-class values and middle-class child-rearing practices. As a matter of fact, the expansion rate of thirty per cent in Brown's records came from academic parents (McNeill 1966:75).

CHARACTERISTICS OF ADULTS' SPEECH TO CHILDREN

The mothers of Kenneth and Mark do not imitate or expand the speech of children to any extent. *However, they do expand their own speech to children.* That is the pattern of speaking to children which the mothers of Rosepoint cannot resist. In its most common form the sentence is repeated three times, varying the total intonation pattern by doubling the volume for successive sentences.

NATALIE: What that is?
PETER: Hunh?
NATALIE: What that is? (*louder*)
PETER: Hunh?
NATALIE: WHAT THAT IS? (*very loud*)

The possible intervening responses of the children are not necessary to the structure.

MOTHER: Get out here.
  Get out here!
  Get out here!!

The above form expanded by intonation (louder each time) is primarily used for questions and imperatives. A more complex and interesting form is the mother's expansion of her own speech into paradigms. Ignoring the child's response, she will continue to paraphrase her own utterances systematically, throwing in a few repetitions for good measure.

> NATALIE: Tell the lady your name.
> Tell the lady your name.
> What your name?
> Tell Joan what your name.
> Tell her your name.
> Tell Joan your name.
> LIZ: Tell Joan your name.
> Tell Joan your name.
> NATALIE: Tell her your mama name.
> What your mama name?

Though all of this was directed at eliciting speech from the child, he squeezed in two "Hunh's" and an "I don't know."

A frequently used form of the mother-to-child paradigm follows this rule. The sentence itself remains intact but surrounded by a changing set of form classes.

$$\left\{ \begin{array}{l} \text{Proper Names} \\ \text{Expletives} \\ \text{Directives} \end{array} \right\} \quad + \quad \text{Sentence} \quad + \quad \left\{ \begin{array}{l} \text{Adverbs} \\ \text{Proper Names} \\ \text{Tag Questions} \end{array} \right\}$$

> What does stop on that track out there?
> Hunh, what does stop on that track out there, Anne?
> Anne, what does stop on that track outside?

In the next set of paradigms another type of alternative is offered, that of internal syntactic substitution.

> Come on back sit on *this* chair.
> Come on come on sit on *that* chair.
> Come on Peter sit on *the* chair.

Here the woman runs through the possibilities for an article modifying a singular noun: *this, that, the.* Any word class can be used. The communicative advantage of this expansion form seems to be a wide variety of syntactic and semantic possibilities with a limited number of lexical items. Moreover, she is graphically presenting his range of syntactic choices.

> And where your Daddy just bring you?
> And where your Daddy just bring you?
> And where   he   just bring you??
>   What   he   bring you?
>   What   he   buy you?
>   What   he   buy you?

> Where you all went Sunday?
> Where you all went Sunday?
> Where did you all go Sunday?

Who brought that sweater to you?
Who brought that pretty sweater?
Who brought that pretty sweater?

What Liz brought you all?
What Liz brought you Anne?
What Liz *bought* you?

What   Scott ate today   for dinner?
What   you ate   for dinner?
What did you eat   for dinner?
What you and Warren have   for dinner?

Sometimes the group of mothers will chime in to complete the paradigm. Women speak in this manner to any children, not just their own.

NATALIE: What your daddy got in his car?
           What your daddy went and put in his car?
CHILD: Soul brother.
LIZ: That what my daddy went and put in his car, eh?

The sentences may be complex with dependent clauses, or they may switch from interrogative to declarative forms. Often the meaning is duplicated and the syntax varied only slightly. A minimal number of lexical items are needed. In the following exchange the same sentence (italicized) is repeated three times, varied somewhat, and accompanied by many extra directions.

1. Come on back here. And let's *talk. Come on you all gonna hear you all voice* on that tape recorder, hear, come on.
2. On that tape recorder. *Come on* sit down and *talk* and then *you all gonna hear your voice* on there.
3. Well come see. *Come on.* Sit down there and *say something* and she gonna play it and *you gonna hear your voice.*

This is maximal redundancy. Between (1) and (2) and between (2) and (3) the child says "hunh?" To an outsider, the mother appears to talk at, rather than with the child. But talk she does.

In the event he does not understand or respond to a question with an inverted verb, she may give him a declarative with interrogative intonation or further variations on this theme.

The one sleep with you, what his name?
Who sleep with you?
Who you sleep with?
What your other brother name is?
What the other one name was sleep with you?

Some recurring patterns in this adult–child speech are best described by designating their rhyme schemes. The systematic repetitiveness of the sentences allows such an interpretation. The following might be called an ABA pattern.

NATALIE: I ain't gonna bring them nowhere,
                    They don't wanna sing
                 I ain't bringing them nowhere.
                 I ain't gonna bring you all in the car,
                    Now if you all don't start talking,
                 I ain't bring you in the car.

This is a highly stylized threat which points up the rhythmic nature of the language used to children. Such forms exist less often in adults' speech to adults. "Lord have mercy! Jesus have mercy! Have mercy!" is one similar form, though most often abbreviated. Some of the mother–child interactions are constructed like spirituals or folksongs in which the rhythms have an hypnotic effect on the participants. The intellectual content is subordinated to the mode of presentation.

NATALIE: Now tell her what you do all day.
                 What do you do in the day?
                 What you do in the day?
                 What you do in the day?
                 You play?
                 Tell her that.
                 Tell her you play.
                 Tell her that!
                 Tell her you play!

If expansions of speech provide the models and the alternatives to facilitate the child's discovery of grammatical features, then these children experience a variety of expanded speech. Not their own but an adult's sentences are expanded. The syntactic models are available in any case. The children of poor factory workers and the children of university graduate students will learn the syntactic rules appropriate to their parents and peers. Along with different dialect, however, they may learn different *sociolects,* or the social uses of language and one's own participation in it.

> It is possible that the behavior of the lower-class parent is not simply a function of diminished motivation and interest in the child's communication but might reflect important differences in systems of information exchange characteristic of this group. Linguistic competence, in the usual sense, may not be as useful to the lower-class child as other communication operations (Chase 1966:259).

THE CONTRAST OF ADULT-TO-ADULT SPEECH

The expansions of sentences are not the usual manner in which adults address other adults and mature teenagers. Compare the following tape transcript with the mother's speech to children. The interview concerns the mother's reaction to her children's use of unacceptable language. Another woman is present but does not speak in this section of the tape.

INVESTIGATOR: What do you do if one of your kids says a dirty word?
ROSA: Nothing.

INVESTIGATOR: Nothing. Really?

ROSA: Because I had my other two in school, they used to say them.

INVESTIGATOR: What did they say?

ROSA: All sorts of dirty words.

INVESTIGATOR: Did they pick them up from the other children?

ROSA: And maybe from me too. Sometime I get mad but what I like about it, now as soon as they gets old enough to understand that it isn't right, they stop it. And whenever they will hear someone else say one, you know, you heard it so-and-so said bad word. Whereas now they would probably come in off the street, you know, and when they was smaller, they probably repeat it, but now they don't ever come to me and repeat it, or nothing of the kind. You see, as they growing old, is grown, they don't say it, regardless of who they hear say it. Uh-hunh, without me having to tell 'em anything. Where I think if you was get on them and brutalize them or beat them it just make them retaliate, get mad or something, they probably would say it just to make you mad. They gotta say it for someone else to hear.

INVESTIGATOR: You know they'll grow out of it then?

ROSA: I know they will, because I have two that have. I think Cicero was even worse than anyone of them. He used to be horrible. And you'll never get Cicero, not even out playing to say bad, using obscene language. And if any of the other kids would say them he will say, oh, he was playing in the front, he don't never come out and say the words. Cause, you know, he say "No I don't know what you saying." But most of the things he do, lots of people think is wrong that I would let, cause I would let him get by with it. But I know my aunt _____ don't love him as much as I do. She never tell them anything. Lots of mothers brutalize their children and really try to chastize them and be hard on them. They have nothing funny, cause those children grew up to hate them and I, we, could see that. They do anything to hurt their mother. I don't know if you call that seeking revenge from their younger days or what.

Compared to this same mother's speech to her children, this segment is free of paralinguistic and marked intonational features. Other differences are easily seen. False starts, communication securing devices such as "you know," and multi-syllabic lexical items such as *brutalize* or *retaliate* are not characteristic of speech to children. She uses tenses other than the present tense. The content, that is, the ideas expressed, is repetitive. For example, the notion that punitive mothers raise children who will grow up to hate them is repeated. This paraphrasing does not resemble the immediate paradigmatic sentence expansions directed to children.

The mean sentence length for adult–child speech is 5.5 words per sentence; the mean sentence length for adult–adult speech is 15.5 words per sentence.[2] This is clearly a substantial differential. The mother is gearing the complexity and length of her sentences to her audience. To her children she uses only a rare relative or subordinate clause ("Now tell her what you do all day"). To the adults she addresses, complex sentences are predominant ("Whereas now they would probably come in off the street, you know, and when they was smaller, they probably repeat it but now they don't ever come to me and repeat it, or nothing of the kind.").

---

[2] Mean sentence length is a numerical average calculated on all expansions of adult–child speech recorded in this chapter; the mean sentence length for the adult–adult speech is calculated from the preceding transcript of Rosa's discussion of swearing and blasphemy.

This type of language usage is overheard by all children; two preschoolers were present at this taping. However, the above language sample is not aimed directly at children. The mother's idea of speech suitable for interaction with children is carefully regularized, as though she were aware that children need precise, workable models of their language.

CORRECTIONS AND REQUESTS FOR INFORMATION

To correct a child's syntax or pronunciation implies some feeling that there is a standard for language, a common "correct" goal toward which all must move. Furthermore, corrections imply that one knows the reason for using one form rather than another, and that one's social setting furnishes a rationalization for "correctness." This is not the case for all social groups. Some people may value improvisation, content, social appropriateness (for example, Japanese politeness terms), or even quantity above correctness of syntax and pronunciation. Even if such a standard is employed, the task of imparting it may not fall to the parents.

Corrections used by the parents under consideration here always center around the standard of behavior and not around the standards of language. Only one grammatical correction is recorded; none are recorded for pronunciation.

CHILD: My mama work to Kaiser.
AUNT: Susie, your mama work at Kaiser. That to New Orlean.

Under these circumstances it is questionable whether the child learned the preposition in question. The following is more typical:

CHILD: Give me two meat.
MOTHER: Two meats! You don't never eat what I give you anyway. You leave it on the plate.

"Two meat" and "two meats" are common alternates, though the former is more often heard. Although the mother unconsciously altered the plural morpheme, its correction as such was of no concern to her. The child's behavior patterns in eating are the focus.

When a child asks a question or volunteers a statement, it will be judged on its behavioral import and not on the structure of the language employed. A child's requests for information are not treated as a demand for knowledge (which adults are expected to supply) or as an attempt to open the lines of communication. Instead, requests are viewed as a behavioral and not a linguistic manifestation of the child. A child actively engaged in seeking information will be treated as a noisy child, not as an inquiring, curious one. As a side effect of being noisy, he may or may not acquire the information he wants.

An insurance adjustor is examining a bedroom damaged by fire.

CHILD: Who that?
FATHER: None of your business!

CHILD: Sarah, what lane you live on?

MOTHER: [*Laughs*] Child, that funny, what lane do Sarah live on. [*This is an affectionate, pleasant interchange but not an opportunity to distinguish lanes and streets.*]

MOTHER: Kenneth want to ask the questions. Once he get started on them, boy, asking questions.

INVESTIGATOR: What other questions does he ask?

MOTHER: Oh boy! What this for? What that for? Most the time, he already know. He say "What are these things?" I tell him, "a horse." "A horse, what that for?" or "What it do?" or something like that. Anything you say, he want to know what it for, what it do. And once he gets started . . . And he don't want to talk when it's time to talk. That boy talks so much! OH! I be whip him all the time all the time.

WHO ARE THE TEACHERS?

The mothers do not feel a very heavy responsibility for language instruction. Neither do they expect to gain prestige through the accomplishments of their children. The level of social achievement for preschoolers is very low in this respect. Such children are not expected to exhibit any range of manners, skills, or special knowledge, that is, talents which can be demonstrated for the benefit of admiring friends and relatives. They are responsible only for taking care of themselves and for following orders. By the time they enter school the children are accomplished at child care, household tasks, and sibling relations. They are responsible for their own whereabouts. However, many may not possess the peripheral skills schools regard as important, such as skill in recitations or pencil and paper facility.

Three of the mothers in this study were picked as teachers' aides for the parish Head Start Program. After the orientation session they expressed considerable surprise at what they were told was the pupils' low level of achievement. Some children, they were informed, did not know the names and identity of colors, numbers, shapes, or animals. This, of course (the mothers were convinced), could not apply to their children, since they were certain such skills had been mastered.

As it turns out, it is the special province of older children to impart the type of knowledge that requires drill. Unlike many middle-class mothers, the women of Rosepoint spend no time drilling their children on such cultural content as the sounds cows make ("moo"), or what happened to Humpty-Dumpty. One mother learned a game in Head Start for teaching children to write their names by following the dots made for them on a piece of paper. She came home, taught three of her school-age children who could already write, and they were gradually teaching the preschoolers! To date, none of the younger children can write their names, but the mother is not only convinced that they can, but that she taught them how.

Many simple (and relatively ineffective) learning drills are conducted between older and younger children. The oldest child present is the teacher—a role learned from older children and not from parents or from experience. In the following tape transcript the children are reading a book containing the alphabet and numbers, for example, "C is for Cat. How many cats are there? Three." The three children are brothers and sisters.

> GWEN: [*Eleven years old*] What is this? What is that?
> MADELAINE: [*Four years old*] I got that toy book.
> GWEN: That's a notebook.
> KENNETH: [*Three years old*] A popcorn maker.
> GWEN: No. What is this—a glass of milk?
>   [*Gwen, as the oldest, is playing the teacher—asking and quizzing. She leaves and Madelaine is the teacher.*]
> MADELAINE: How many is that?
> KENNETH: I don't know.
> MADELAINE: That's a two. See that a two. [*It is an eight.*]
> KENNETH: A two.
> MADELAINE: That's a horse. How much horse they got?
> KENNETH: Two. [*Four horses.*]
> MADELAINE: Look that one. How many kitten they got?
> KENNETH: Cat.
> MADELAINE: No, kitten. How many kitten they got?
> KENNETH: Two.
> MADELAINE: They got three. [*Seven kittens*] How many? How many? How much kitten they got? Kenneth, how much ducks they got?
> KENNETH: Two-oh-oh-oh.
> MADELAINE: Look, one-two-three-four-seven- Now that's a three. An' that's a seven. [*None of these answers is correct.*]

Such prodigious activity persuades the mother that her children are learning much. She will never know that the identification was wrong.

INSTRUCTIVE FUNCTIONS

It has sometimes been asserted in the popular press that black mothers do not talk to their children and that that tendency accounts for the observed differences between black and white students in the public schools.

Compare the conversation with Adam to the ones that follow with Kenneth and Mark. There is almost no subject matter which is initiated by children that adults feel is incumbent upon them to pursue. It is the right of adults to select the topic of conversation. Moreover, adults can conduct a satisfying conversation with only the most minimal feedback. A smile, nod, or "hunh?" is all that is required of a child to uphold his end. The subject matter of Adam's conversation is his own choosing and initiation. The mother's participation tends to be non-directive, and control is exercised in a rather subtle manner.

Adam's mother and the mothers of Kenneth and Mark have different assumptions about the proper sentence form in addressing children. These assumptions stem from their beliefs about the nature of children. The middle-class mother will expand her child's telegraphic offering into a short but grammatical sentence appropriate under the circumstances. "Me go" might become "You want to go?," "Yes, we are going now," or "Oh, you went to the store," depending on her evaluation of the situation.

The Rosepoint mother imitates and expands her own utterances. The child is a passive recipient of both the models and the data, as in her child-rearing philosophy he should be. The probable drawback to learning a language under these circumstances is the lack of individualized adjustment to whatever stage of grammatical development the child has reached. The mother's speech is not tailor-made to the child's linguistic maturity. By contrast, Adam's mother renders fuller sentences made to order on the child's own model.

ADAM: There go one.
MOTHER: Yes, there goes one.

Fortrel's mother offers him similar and more sophisticated possibilities. But her paradigms appear to bear little relationship to the structures he may already have mastered.

FORTREL'S MOTHER: What you ate for dinner?
What did you eat for dinner?

These differences result from the respective parents' beliefs about their role in language instruction. Fortrel's mother does not view herself as a language instructor nor her child as a budding conversationalist. After all, her child will learn to talk—all children within her experience have. She is concerned about his overt behavior, not his speaking ability.

Few family systems in the world are so constructed that the child is exposed almost exclusively to his mother's speech. The American middle class has this type of isolated, nuclear family. The initial research on language acquisition, perhaps as an artifact of the data, tended to give major emphasis to the role of the mother in language socialization. From information collected from field workers in a symposium on communicative competence (Slobin 1968:9–13), only the Mayan family system, of those considered, exhibited the same characteristics as the American nuclear family. Here, as in the American middle-class home, the mother is the chief source of input. For the Koya of India, the Luo of Kenya, and the Polynesians of American Samoa, the most important source of input to children was from peers, siblings, and the members of an extended family (Slobin 1968:9–13). The tendency seems to be that those with control over the children, having caretaking responsibilities, provide the most input.

The situation most analgous to Rosepoint comes from a Negro ghetto in Oakland.

> Most of the speech of mothers to children . . . took the form of imperatives or such questions as *Where are your shoes, Are you hungry,* etc. . . . . The artificiality of mother to child conversation beyond what has been mentioned is underscored by many mothers' limitations in eliciting speech from their children at the request of the investigator. Mothers were hard put to engage a child in conversation beyond naming games for younger children and requests for reporting about particular events, such as what went on in nursery school for older children. In other words, they suffered from many of the same limitations as the investigator who was unfamiliar with the children and their attempts to engage their children in conversation were for the most part abortive (Slobin 1968:12).

If the mother is not the only source of input, who else is? Other adults are not, since either, as in the case of tradesmen, they do not speak to the children, or, as in the case of family friends, they duplicate the mother's type of speech. In view of the above anthropological observations, it is likely that the peer and sibling group are an important source of input. In an extended family with many children whose neighbors are extended families with many children, one primary linguistic resource is probably other children, siblings, and cousins.

This is difficult to demonstrate. The mere presence of an adult investigator ruins the composition and changes the atmosphere of a peer group, particularly preschoolers. Testifying from personal experience, it is extremely hard to spy on the in-group activities of small children and virtually impossible to do so with a tape recorder. The study of peer-group linguistic interaction needs a more controlled setting than a crowded, noisy, rural Louisiana home provides.

Most of what adults and parents in Rosepoint say to children is *administrative speech*—that speech necessary to conduct the business of the day. Administrative speech consists mainly of orders, questions, and short answers. The total amount of speech directly aimed at the child could not possibly account for the complexities of the grammar he is learning. However compensatory peer-group speech may be, it does not approach the adult model. It is probable that the speech of the peer group merely reinforces and imitates what each age grade learns about the adult community model and allows an opportunity for practice.

Meanwhile, for the children of this community the time spent in the presence of adults is spent passively listening. This statement makes no guarantee that the children hear anything; how the language is comprehended and processed is yet a mystery. At any rate, the children spend most of every day within earshot of every type of speech event the community has to offer. This might be called an eavesdropping theory of language learning. Language learning in Rosepoint differs in this respect from that of a community in which a child receives more formal language training in the home but has less chance to observe a wide range of adult behavior.

A THEORETICAL PROBLEM

The verbal reactions of the mothers in Rosepoint present a fascinating theoretical problem. How do children learn their language and its rules in the absence of conscious instruction? Obviously these caretakers do not believe that they are "teaching" children to speak. Teaching here means the formal and observable attempts to impart certain structures, words, or concepts as well as corrections and judgments of the truth value of children's early utterances. In learning philosophies from Dewey to Skinner, great emphasis is placed on the role of verbal instruction and imitations of the parent by the child. In stimulus-response theories the child is rewarded for producing utterances which presumably he has borrowed from his elders. In Rosepoint, however, in a natural setting rather than an experimental one, children imitate adults far less frequently than adults imitate themselves. Furthermore, the parents pay no conscious attention to their role in assisting language learning.

Consider the possibility that children's language comes from their own maturational development and is not just a response to purposive, rewarding speech from adults. This generative, or biologically based theory of language acquisition is described in Lenneberg, (1966; 1967); McNeill (1966); and Lyons and Wales (1966).

According to this theory, language development involves such qualitative features as phonological discrimination (as in the differences between *b* and *p*, *t* and *d*), syntactic rules (as in "I am," "you are," "he ain't"), and semantic categories (as in "man," "Daddy," "Father," "person"). No differences in the age or speed of acquisition of these features can be found in cultures studied thus far (Lenneberg 1967:138). That is, unless deaf, pathologically diseased, or otherwise seriously handicapped, the average five-year old has mastered most of the sound system, the syntax, and many of the semantic categories of his language.

A corollary of this theory is that so-called linguistically deprived children do not exist. Certain children lack a familiarity with rhymes, stories, linguistic routines, colors, shapes, numbers, specialized vocabularies, dates, time telling, reading, writing, spelling, approved past tenses or other skills that are the core of formal education; but speak they can. It is a mistake to confuse the set of verbal skills, including notions of "correct grammar," which are measured by a limited set of intelligence and achievement tests with a child's *language*.

Naturally, regular differences in syntax and word forms exist for different experience groups, but the basic process of acquisition is still the same. The process by which one child derives "he do"——"he do not"——"he don't"—— "don't he" is the same process that another child uses to derive a chain ending for "doesn't he." It is only the social context that renders "don't he" less acceptable than "doesn't he."

What parent says to her child, "Add an /-s/ to all third-person singular present-tense verbs."? She may correct "he go" to "he goes," but even with this unusual coaching, the child must himself generalize these rules to extend to all words which he has further learned to classify as verbs. The complicated rule systems which a child can generate and the implications of this are also described in Berko (1958); Weir (1962); Menyuk (1964); and Bellugi (1965).

Any theory of language learning would have to explain Rosepoint in which the children appear to receive little formal instruction and even less practice in their emerging skills.

6/Keeping them children under control

NATALIE: Come sit on that chair. Get that flyswatter, kill those flies. Come on, get from under the table now and sit down and you talk. Come on Peter. Come on now. Come on. Get from under the table.
CHILD: No.
NATALIE: You know. He won't get from under the table and sit down.
LIZ: Get from under that table. Come on!!
NATALIE: Now sit on that chair side and sing.
FORTREL: Hunh?
NATALIE: Sit on that chair side, Fortrel. Now what you going to sing.
FORTREL: Hunh?
NATALIE: Sit on that chair side, Fortrel. Now what you going to say?
FORTREL: Hunh?
NATALIE: What you going to sing? You all ain't bashful.
FORTREL: Hunh?

Previous chapters were devoted to a discussion of the extended family structure found in Rosepoint. Economic and physical survival for the many children in these families takes precedence over creative development. The men, if not unemployed, have jobs with very low incomes. Crowded homes, inadequate schools, racial discrimination, and the rural environment foster communal values over individual achievement. However, a tightly woven web of community participation, mutual aid, and the continuity of generations ready to help contribute richly to family life.

A social structure such as that postulated in this chapter engenders its own form of language practices. The casual relationship between family structure and linguistic interaction is the proposal of a British sociologist, Basil Bernstein (1964;1968a). In his theory, the role systems of various types of families generate procedures of social control. As social control is primarily enforced through the medium of language, the linguistic input to children varies from family system to family system with the form of social control. The general result of these family interaction patterns is to create separate languages or "codes" between classes. That there are gross differences between lower-class and middle-class communication is well recognized (Schatzman and Strauss 1966:443).

What factors in the social structure could produce these differences in communication styles?

If a social group, by virtue of its class relation, that is, as a result of its common occupational function and social status, has developed strong communal bonds;

if the work relations of this group offers little variety; little exercise in decision-making; if assertion, if it is to be successful, must be a collective rather than an individual act; if the work task requires physical manipulation and control rather than symbolic organization and control; if the diminished authority of the man at work is transformed into an authority of power at home; if the home is over-crowded and limits the variety of situations it can offer; if the children socialise each other in an environment offering little intellectual stimuli; if all these attributes are found in one setting, then it is plausible to assume that such a social setting will generate a particular form of communication which will shape the intellectual, social and affective orientation of the children (Bernstein 1968a:2).

The hypothetical family system described above resembles Rosepoint. This kind of organization has been called the positional family because one's status or position in the group determines the form communication will take. The contrast to this is the personalized family system, named for the emphasis on the individual's unique communication.

PERSONAL AND POSITIONAL FAMILIES

The following are characterisics of person-oriented families. Achieved status is stronger than ascribed status. Parents are sensitive to the uniqueness of *each* of their children, and child-rearing methods are predicated largely on the inherent differences of their children. Age or sex is less important than personality characteristics. In these families children increasingly play a role as an individual in the community rather than as a five-year-old female of the family X. "Looked at from another point of view, the children would be socializing the parents as much as the parents were socializing the children" (Bernstein 1968a:20). Roles are not rigidly assigned, and hence there is room for innovation as well as ambiguity. Because of the necessity for verbalizing individual preferences, feelings, and judgments, this is an open communication system.

According to Bernstein, positional families have a more closed communication system in which a member's status carries more weight than do personality characteristics. Familial roles are strictly segregated. For children status is determined by age and sex classification and is not a matter for verbal negotiation. Socialization is unilateral inasmuch as individual differences are not verbally elaborated to form a basis for child-rearing techniques. There is little or no need to explore verbally the in or outs of separate psyches. The child adjusts to a succession of status requirements. His membership in a family or community, rather than any individually achieved categorization, offers him less choice of alternatives and less ambiguous, more structured role relationships. The social role determines the verbal repertoire; the child does not need to manipulate his social environment verbally to find a place.

The linguistic consequences of the open and closed family communicative systems can be seen in the example of social control. Though sheer physical power may be the last resort, social control can still be enforced linguistically. In the person-oriented family language is the conscious means of arbitration, explanation, punishment-reward, and just plain coping. The family must very early sensitize the child to the verbal means of social control. In positional families there is no verbal jockeying for new favors and status because pre-existent norms define behavior. Therefore, the verbal means of social control can be minimized simply by appealing to these status norms and expectations. For example, a "position-oriented" mother would say, "Don't hit your baby brother. Stop it." She is communicating notions of authority and status. A "person-oriented" mother would say, "This poor baby can't do all the fun things you can. Don't be jealous of him," or "Why don't you try hitting this stuffed animal instead of the baby?," or "Your father and I love you just as much as this new baby." This mother is communicating emotions (jealousy, aggression, love). The above examples of the person-oriented mother are suggested by a psychologists's description of the properly verbalizing middle-class mother in *Between Parent and Child* (Ginott 1968).

APPEALS

In a sociological study of 351 London families, reasearchers presented imaginary situations to mothers of young children (Bernstein and Young 1968; Robinson, n.d.). To a question like "What would you do if your child stole some flowers for you?" the mothers were asked to indicate what they would say and do. The first category, what the mother reported *saying*, is called appeals. Appeals are verbal messages designed to effect a behavior change in the child. The second category, strategies, are the actions taken in controlling children. All of this material comes from interviews, not from direct observation of the actual situation.

Positional-oriented appeals are geared to status, position, and a relative lack of choice. Linguistically, they take the form of rules which mothers repeat to their children.

Universal rules: moral laws which are no respecter of persons. "It's a sin to lie."
Status rules: the laws of age, sex, age relations, and institutional authority. "Little girls don't sit like that." "Children have to learn to respect their parents." "Teachers won't put up with that sort of behavior."
Family rules: "In our family we always do such-and-such."
Limited rules: rules which refer to specific places and events—a catch-all category. "Take care of yourself." "Be good."

In the category of personal appeals, the child's behavior is explained to him in terms of its effect on himself, his parents, or someone else. The consequences may be explained before or after the act, or both. The affective quality or intent of the child is emphasized. Does he wish to create such an emotion in himself and others? Here may follow more information about the consequences of a given action. Some of these statements are powerful emotional appeals to consequences far beyond the immediate.

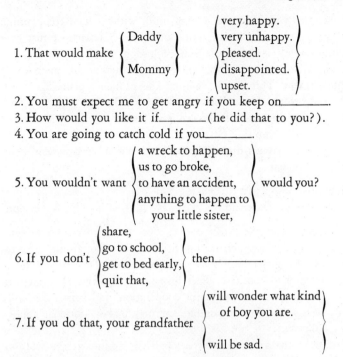

1. That would make $\left\{\begin{array}{c}\text{Daddy}\\\\\text{Mommy}\end{array}\right\}$ $\left\{\begin{array}{l}\text{very happy.}\\\text{very unhappy.}\\\text{pleased.}\\\text{disappointed.}\\\text{upset.}\end{array}\right\}$

2. You must expect me to get angry if you keep on_____.

3. How would you like it if_____(he did that to you?).

4. You are going to catch cold if you_____.

5. You wouldn't want $\left\{\begin{array}{l}\text{a wreck to happen,}\\\text{us to go broke,}\\\text{to have an accident,}\\\text{anything to happen to}\\\quad\text{your little sister,}\end{array}\right\}$ would you?

6. If you don't $\left\{\begin{array}{l}\text{share,}\\\text{go to school,}\\\text{get to bed early,}\\\text{quit that,}\end{array}\right\}$ then_____.

7. If you do that, your grandfather $\left\{\begin{array}{l}\text{will wonder what kind}\\\quad\text{of boy you are.}\\\\\text{will be sad.}\end{array}\right\}$

The nature of these appeals vary from guilt to common sense but center around the reactions of the child and other people. Sometimes in the personal category, appeals can be very subtle. For example, if one wants something from a child, he holds out a hand and says "thank you." "Thank you" is a request which may be met by the child. As a polar type, the most extreme form of positional appeals is an imperative: "Give me that thing." What a child learns about the use of language is obviously different in the two instances. This classification of appeals is adapted from Bernstein et al. (1968b).

STRATEGIES AND MANIPULATION

Strategies are concerned with what actions the mother must take in controlling her child. What the mother does, not what she says, is the criterion. Still, unarticulated attitudes about child-rearing influence language development too.

Some problems are never defined into existence and hence no action is necessary. In Rosepoint, sibling rivalry as a category of behavior and a potential problem is not recognized. One little girl is said to be jealous of her smaller cousin, but this is understood as an attribute of that family structure and certainly not as an emotion or situation to which any child is exposed at the birth of a sibling. Perhaps because jealousy remains unnamed, childhood seems free of sibling frictions.

Where a problem is known to exist a mother may take routine nonaction, responding perfunctorily and minimizing the incident. Mopping up spills, changing the clothes of wet two year olds, and wiping noses without loud complaining are ways of recognizing problems without acting on them. This lack of fuss over the minutiae of child-rearing is the prevailing philosophy in Rosepoint.

Anticipatory action, diversionary action, and ritualized action are methods of control short of punishment. This means defining the problem, planning in advance sometimes to the extent of establishing a ritual for dealing with it. Carrying toys in the purse, insisting on a bathroom visit before a trip, and reading a story before bedtime are examples.

Punishment in Rosepoint covers direct physical and verbal chastisement, commands, threats, and banishment.

Commands: "Shut up!" "Stop that." "Don't." "No!"
Categoric repetitions: "He'd better do it." "I'd make him do it." "He better not."

This sort of social control is the direct opposite of the mother-child orientation in which coaxing, wheedling, persuading, bribing, and bargaining are employed. These fall into the general category of concessions. The mother offers rewards instead of punishment—positive affect instead of negative. She agrees to relax a rule, offers a privilege in exchange for cooperation, and bribes the child with threats. Since rewards are often intangible, she may make emotional appeals to love, shame, and guilt.

One indication of positionalized vis-à-vis personalized families is the wording of statements used to rationalize child-rearing philosophies. Mothers who are

Children playing with a kitten.

position oriented may use collective nouns or pronouns such as *we, they, children, people, boys, girls,* or unconditional phrases such as *usually,* or *always.* Proverbs and clichés are frequent. Personalized statements would be marked by proper names, personal pronouns, *I, you, he, she,* and conditional statements such as *if . . . then* and *it depends.*

Another technique for recognizing positionalized and personalized philosophies is the examination of parents' actual verbalizations in controlling children. This includes observing the occurrence of threats, imperatives, appeals, tricking, and disciplinary measures.

THREATS

Two categories of threats apply to children in Rosepoint:

1. Substantive warnings which carry meaningful penalties;
2. Invectives or imprecations which sound frightening but have no immediate consequences.

Within the first category the threats are capable of being realized. "You gonna see what I lay on you;" or "You want me to whip you," are not rhetorical statements. A spanking follows if immediate compliance is not forthcoming.

"I'm ona $\begin{Bmatrix} \text{beat} \\ \text{whip} \\ \text{spank} \end{Bmatrix}$ you."

"I'm gonna pop the hell out of you."

These are not idle threats but announcements of impending action.

Other such threats include withdrawal of privileges. As the children are obsessed with riding in cars, this can be effective. The mother never employs this threat as a bribe or for bargaining purposes. In other words, she does not say: "If you'll do such-and-such, I'll take you riding." In this statement a child may be enjoined from performing a prescribed act or encouraged in some coveted behavior. However, the wording of this phrase is a direct bribe. When he does something for his mother, she does something for him. Changing this statement into a negative eliminates the bribe and substitutes the threat: "If you do not do such-and-such, I won't take you riding." "If . . . then" statements directed to children in Rosepoint typically take the latter form of threats, not of bribes.

When enough misdemeanors and the petty irritations of children accumulate, the mother may suddenly say, "I'm not bringing you riding." The desired effect is not to correct some specific behavior pattern such as interrupting when company is present, playing with the food, or making messes but to prevent him from further "worrying my nerve." She expects him to withdraw. Later she may or may not carry out the threat. The mother who threatened not to take Desiree to the game (page 16) was threatening ride deprivation. She did, however, take the child to the game.

Children are never threatened with withdrawal of food, affection, or companionship. Isolation as a punishment ("go to your room") is almost an environmental impossibility.

The other category of threats is just as serious but does not imply actual disciplinary consequences, for example,

"I'm going to kill you."

Standard variations on this sentence include the following:

"I'm going to choke you."
"I'm going to shoot you."
"I'm going to hang you."

All of these are exact quotes. Parents repeat them constantly, sometimes improvising on the method they intend to use.

The threats are not as farfetched as they sound. In the local folklore are stories about mothers who did, in fact, kill their children. One woman strangled her six-month-old infant because she did not want it. Another woman (the storyteller's distant consanguineal relative) locked her four children in the house and burned it down. No proof of arson exists, but her lack of remorse was so interpreted. Though this is gossip, the alleged evildoers are quickly acquiring the status of local witches. People are afraid to drive by their houses. As children hear all the gossip in the community, they are not spared these stories either. No *overt* indication exists that they fear such retaliation. However, the fright value of these threats coupled with stories of children who met such fate may be an excellent buttress to an authoritarian system of social control.

Once in a while supernatural threats are utilized. Attempting to move a recalcitrant niece, aged two, who was sitting in the middle of the lane and refused to budge, the aunt said, "Come on, get up, let's go." The child refused. She did not say anything, just sat. "O.K. If you sit there the boogie man get you." The child was unmoved. "A car going to come and run over you." Still no results. Finally, the aunt went over and picked up the child.

Another mother favors, "God going to punish bad children." This threat is apparently tied to the theological belief that life and death are "God's will"— a sophistication which leaves the children unaffected.

IMPERATIVES AND APPEALS

In Rosepoint imperatives are the primary form of verbal manipulation. Simple, direct, and unambiguous commands may be the only verbal contact between mother and child for hours on end:

"Catch me that brush."
"Turn on the T. V."
"Go on outside."
"Shut up."

One type of imperatives is reserved for special occasions.

MOTHER: Give me that purse. [*normal tone*]
Give me that purse!! [*very much louder*]
GIVE ME THAT PURSE! [*yelling*]

Lynel, go on, get outside.
Go on, get outside, Lynel!!
GO ON, GET OUTSIDE!

In this form of repetition the central sentence conveying the message retains its same syntactic structure for three successive times. Proper names and curses may be added to either end of the sentences. Within this simple structure a wide variety of poetic effects can be achieved. The "operatic" patterns for each sentence are indicated by the punctuation marks; each sentence must be repeated twice as loud as the preceding but with the same intonation pattern. Although the children know that this little chant is a command to be taken seriously, they usually stay for the end of the performance. It is a satisfying ritual.

Commands are the standard form of manipulation within the positional family system. Many of the imperatives may have an unarticulated rule reinforcing them. For instance, this is true of the household tasks which children assume increasingly from age four. If the child fails to perform the task, the mother reminds him by giving a louder, firmer order, but does not remind him that a family rule exists setting forth this job for him.

Besides naked references to authority, the appeals to status, age, and age grading are the major vehicle of coercion. A mother spots her three-year-old son, four-year-old daughter, and three-year-old niece playing in the car of the next door neighbor. She calls to them: "I guess you want me to whip you!" They run home immediately because her yell is not an idle threat. As the children enter the door, she takes a hearty whack at each, but misses the first two so she spanks the last one through. This is her four-year-old daughter who says:

GIRL: I told Kenneth stay home.
MOTHER: Don't tell me you told Kenneth.
You the oldest.
Pull that again and I'll hang you.

The appeal to age status, relative or not, is very strong. The four-year-old girl is the oldest of this particular group, so she is responsible. The feeble attempts to talk her mother out of the expected punishment are clearly unsuccessful. Neither does the mother give clear indications as to what the child could have done or should do the next time this happens—except to act as the oldest. Presumably the child tried to do this and failed.

At another time the same mother is trying to persuade this little girl to play outside. The company inside is more fascinating.

MOTHER: Go outside.
Go outside!!
GO OUTSIDE!
Your brother outside, and he younger then you.

She means that if her brother is outside, the little girl should be too. The little girl is not the baby of the family. When the child is unmoved by these appeals, the mother picks her up bodily, sets her outside, and locks the door. The appeal to status and the physical removal represent the mother's second and third efforts, respectively, at dismissing the child. Her first try had been a series of accelerating imperatives. Usually, these alone have the desired effect.

Another mother makes a series of status appeals concerning her youngest. To her other children she says, "Don't hit my baby." "Take my baby with you." This little boy is always "her baby," not "your little brother or cousin" or "the baby." The appeal is to the child's absolute status as *her* baby, age two and a half, and not to his position in the family hierarchy relative to the person to whom she is speaking.[1]

The most frequent category of appeals is to age, either relative to the age grading system or in absolute terms. Appeals to sex status, that is, a son or daughter, boy or girl, are much less frequent than to age. Although appeals sometimes blur into rationales, one category of status appeals is clear in light of the theory of the positional family, that is, appeals to poverty.

> MADELAINE: [*Volunteers*] I don't go to kindergarten.
> INVESTIGATOR: You don't?
> MADELAINE: My mama don't want me to.
> MOTHER: You got that wrong. It ain't a matter of want. I can't afford it. It cost fifteen dollars a month. We too poor.

> LITTLE BOY: Momma, buy me some gum.
> MOTHER: I done bought you some gum, yeah. I can't afford no more.

> MOTHER: Buy me this, buy me that, you think I be rich, yeah. [*This is a response to a child's request for candy or other goodies.*]

These are appeals to the economic status of the family. As families push their buying power to the limit, taking advantage of all available credit, of the generosity of relatives and perhaps of part time jobs, the statement "We too poor" is the judgment from which there is no appeal.

In Rosepoint a child is not told that his behavior has psychological effects on his parents (making them happy, unhappy, pleased, sad, and so forth) or that the consequences of his misbehavior are anything more than a whipping, tongue-lashing, or denial of a car ride. He is not responsible for the emotional state of his parents or for the consequences of his actions beyond the immediate time and place.

---

[1] Note that this status terminology tends to center the family around the mother. This can be contrasted with the Japanese reference patterns which center around the youngest child (Fischer 1964:115–126).

DISCIPLINARY ACTIVITIES

One of the functions of language in manipulation is to transfer time from the past or into the future. This time transfer in language could be particularly important in social control where the lessons of the past are conjured up to delineate the experiences of the present or the future, or where fear of the future motivates the present. To what extent is discipline time-oriented? The following sample sentences are collected from essentially middle-class situations: family comedies on television, novels, and from families known to the author. They are not typical of disciplinary utterances in Rosepoint.

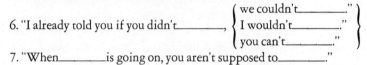

1. "How many times { have I told you not to_____?"
                   { do I have to tell you not to_____?" }

2. "I thought it was decided that_____."
3. "You know you're not supposed to_____."
4. "I'm going to tell your father when he gets home."
5. "Next time, do such-and-such."
6. "I already told you if you didn't_____, { we couldn't_____."
                                               { I wouldn't_____."
                                               { you can't_____." }
7. "When_____is going on, you aren't supposed to_____."

The blanks can be filled in with any subject negotiated by parents and children. Use of this type of language in socialization depends on (1) personalized relationships: "I," "you," "we," and (2) a well-defined categorization of the "good" and "bad" acts of children. This is the only way the blanks can be filled in properly. Families adept at this method have in effect imparted a generalized code of conduct with the misdemeanors properly named and the rewards and punishments spelled out. In this disciplinary system, parents wanting to make the punishment fit the crime may go to bizarre lengths. A child will not be punished for a transgression that does not have a name. Instead, he is warned, "The next time you do X (this undesirable behavior), I will have to_____ (some punitive response)." And when it happens again, "I told you last time you did X, that I was going to_____." Moreover, he will be told that "X is bad because_____," and will be given the rationale for classifying these activities and administering the punishment. The episode is usually concluded with a generalized principle for future behavior: "In the future, remember, good little boys don't X!"

Contrast this with a discipline system which is not anticipatory, does not deal in principles, classifications, or esoteric reward and punishments. Instead we have a system in which the punishments are both *immediate* and *well-defined*. Either the child goes scot-free or he is promptly spanked, "cussed out," or deprived of a very limited class of privileges. Moreover, the statute of limitations is short. The child is not deprived tomorrow for something he did today. Nor is he threatened with dire and distant future punishments. In a community where all caretakers share in discipline and no place is too public to manage a wayward child, there is no need for anticipating or postponing measures of social control.

Mothers do not carry around with them a catalogue of childhood sins. When asked why a child was punished, the answer is "he a cheeky bastard," or "she got ugly ways." The particular action which brought this fact to the mother's attention is not mentioned. In other words, he is not punished for "doing X" which is "bad." Mothers do not have to classify to their children or to any other person activities deserving of punishment.

Children are punished for crying, bothering their mother, and not obeying orders such as "shut up," "go outside," or "stop acting (up)."

> MOTHER: [*To four year old*] No! You can't go in the car. What you crying for? I give you something to cry about. [*Whop.*]

Crying, *per se*, elicits no sympathy, whereas the cause of it may, if injury or pain result. Crying without reason is a punishable offense. If the offender is lucky, his wailing is ignored.

While children may be punished for crying and making too much noise, they are not responsible for what might be thought of as "linguistic offenses," sassiness, for example. A child who adopts the same tone and phrases as his mother will be laughed at. In keeping with their philosophy of "sticks and stones may break my bones, but words can never hurt me," a child's cursing or profanity is interpreted as funny and will receive the laugh it deserves if done well. This is a paramount case of children being rewarded for creative use of language.

Discipline is not conceived of as a learning process in which a child's repeated misdemeanors are evidence of not having "learned his lesson." Nor does each correction of some infringement necessitate a moral to be drawn, a warning, injunction, or generalization for future conduct. Discipline is to insure an immediate response from the child (getting out from underfoot, being quiet, doing a job) or to punish lack of same. Situations defined as problems are handled the same way every day.

To some extent this disciplinary system is age-graded. As children grow larger, it is no longer possible to pick them up bodily or whip them at will. Language functions must become more sophisticated. An eleven-year-old boy came back from school one day in tears. There was no toilet paper in the school washroom; he had become very messy and the teacher sent him home. His mother screamed at him, cuffed him several times, jerked his clothes off and, while running the bath water said,

> You shit-ass bastard! [*not inappropriate under the circumstances*] Lemme see, get in there and lemme see you take a bath. Why you didn't ask for some? Next time, ask before!!
> NEXT TIME, ASK BEFORE!
> NEXT TIME, ASK BEFORE!!

While "next time, ask before" is not exactly a guiding principle of life, it is a suggestion for future conduct. When asked why she said this, she replied that a boy his age was old enough to understand such ideas. However, she went on, her other children were not old enough and for them she would have omitted the lecture that supplemented the cuffing. Moreover, she would not have asked younger children for an explanation ("why you didn't ask for some?"). Said she, "They don't know no better."

The disciplinary system is best summarized by this mother:

> MOTHER: [*To investigator*] I told that child to clean the bathroom.
> INVESTIGATOR: What if she doesn't?
> MOTHER: *She will. Ain't no such thing as doesn't and won't.*

So the mother goes to the kitchen door and reminds her child again. "Cindy, get in here and clean up this bathroom." Without a word, Cindy does.

VERBAL TRICKS IN MANIPULATION

Manipulation in many families is primarily verbal and would not be strictly speaking disciplinary. Instead, social control is exercised less through physical coercion or threats and more through linguistic means. Verbal tricks are a circuitous route to communicating acceptable forms of behavior to children. The following examples are not from Vacherie. Intended as a contrast to the forms of manipulation already discussed, they were collected from middle-class families.

The polite lie If everything must have a reason, reasons become an end in themselves and the result may be an inadvertent lie.

"It's for your own good."
"Carrots help you see in the dark."
"Food tastes better if you sit in a chair."
"You're a brave boy; this shot won't hurt."

The suggestion Suggestions may have the import, if not the force, of commands.

"How would you like to go outside and play?"
"Wouldn't it be fun to make up our beds?"

The "understanding" statement Anticipating that her child experiences feelings of hate, anger, and guilt, the parent attempts to show his understanding of these emotions. She does not expect conformity to a behavioral ideal but an understanding of the emotions expressed. The basic philosophy is an interest in the process of interaction and not just the end results.

"I know that you want to go out with your father and me tonight, but that is impossible."
"I understand that you feel angry with me."
"Sometimes I feel angry with you."
"Sometimes you hate your little sister and want to hit her, don't you?"

(These sentence types are suggested by Ginott 1965.)

Comparisons   The mother may deny that she intends to compare her child with others. But to the child the intent is clear.

"I see Mrs. So-and-So's daughter is on the Honor Roll."
"Bobby is such a nice little boy, such good manners."

The third-party technique   Messages from the mother are transmitted through the medium of a third person. She has definite ideas to communicate to the child but appears to be speaking to someone else.

"Johnny is really a little helper."
"Mary could do better in school if she really tried, couldn't you, Mary?"

On occasion the message is directed to the third party but channeled through the child. To uphold the charade between adults is all that is expected of the child.

"Show Mrs. Smith how well you use the potty." (The visitor is supposed to compliment this skill.)
"Why don't you take Aunt Jane and show her the closet where she can put her coat."

Teasing   By this joking form of social control, or merely the fear of it, the child is brought into line. Teasing is a method of dealing with the truth without talking directly about it. The rationalizations for teasing as a means of social control are given to the child in a verbal form to justify the below the surface unpleasantness.

"You need to learn to take teasing."
"If you can't take a little teasing, you're never going to have any friends."

The rationale for teasing is an extension of the ploy, "I'm only doing this for your own good." Teasing is one of the most subtle forms of verbal social control.

Many other examples of socialization by purely verbal techniques exist. Sarcasm, appeals to a sense of guilt or shame, or the hint of love's withdrawal and parental displeasure, are instances which the reader may remember from his own childhood or observe in many American homes. The majority of these tactics are the correlate of a public versus a private standard of socialization. In public or in the presence of witnesses the mother feels constrained not to smack or yell at her child. She must resort to suggestions, little lies, veiled threats, teasing, or whatever comprises her repertoire. In the privacy of her home she may not be forced to rely exclusively on such tactics.

In Rosepoint such verbal stratagems are very rare. For one reason, there are no public and private standards of socialization. For another, parents believe that children are so hardheaded that nothing subtle will penetrate. Only the most obvious and direct techniques, it is believed, will work. The effectiveness of any socialization practice is in direct proportion to the mother's volume and motor activity. To get a child to eat his dinner one does not say, "Don't your red beans and rice taste good today?" but "Eat your dinner!!" Obtaining peace and quiet is accomplished by "Get out of here!! Go play outside!!" and not by "It's such a pretty day to play outside." Parents believe that complimenting a child will not spur him on to greater achievements. Manipulating a child by tricking him verbally is not a part of their socialization practices. If they have fault to find or orders to give, a simple statement of blunt honesty will suffice.

CHILDREN'S MANIPULATION OF PARENTS AND OTHER ADULTS

Children are not at all successful at manipulating their parents. The definition of manipulation in this case is best summarized by the popular notion of "being spoiled." A spoiled child has learned how to manipulate his parents. While virtually all children in Rosepoint over the age of one are "bad," they are certainly not "spoiled." Only rich or white people have spoiled children.

Children may attract the attention of their parents by touching them, pulling at their skirts or hands, or asking a question. Simple requests, such as for water, food, a nickel, permission to play outside are responded to immediately with a resounding "NO!" or by a cheerful compliance with the request. Only babes-in-arms are cuddled and kissed, and they have a right to demand this attention. Older children rarely receive such affectionate caresses.

Attempting to dominate or manipulate an adult verbally is equally unproductive. Adults do not regard children as people to talk to. Conversations initiated by children are very short-lived.

MADELAINE: Mama, Mark done drink Rosa cold drink.
MOTHER: Shut up, eat your dinner.

CINDY: I want some ice cream.
MOTHER: Shut up.

KENNETH: What this is? [*Points to picture in book*]
MOTHER: Child, I don't know.

MADELAINE: Can I go cross the field to Susie house?
MOTHER: YOU CAN'T GO NOWHERE!

CHILD: Mama, Mama, Mama!!
MOTHER: Go outside! Go outside!!

(These preceding conversations are taken from tape transcripts.)

All of the children observed are what a middle class adult would term "shy." They do not compete or vie for the attention of adults. Rarely are questions asked or answered or is information volunteered. These interactions are possible only on an extended acquaintance with the children. They usually speak in whispers or low tones which seem all the softer in their noisy environments. The mothers are convinced, nonetheless, that their children talk all the time, and part of their definition of "badness" includes talkativeness. Children are noisy. They roll around, moan, yell, bang things, and laugh but still do not have much to say around adults.

The failure of children to manipulate their parents is most clearly seen in their inability to talk themselves out of punishment. The few feeble attempts witnessed met with a singular lack of success. Many children are clever enough to do so were the opportunity present. However, given the prevailing attitude that children are not punished for the sins of the moment but because they are bad, attempts to mitigate the consequences with words only adds fuel to the fire.

INTERROGATIVE FUNCTIONS

Questioning techniques in linguistic socialization are another phase of adult-child communication and information exchange. Who asks the questions? What kinds of questions are asked? What kind of answers are given?

Children who attempt to manipulate their parents by verbal ploys get nowhere:

CHILD: Mama, who gonna cut the cake?
MOTHER: Child, don't you worry about that.

Even genuine requests for information may not warrant informative replies. For the mother's part, however, questioning is her primary resource in eliciting speech from her child. Direct imperatives, her first inclination, are useless. Outside of administrative speech and imperatives, questions are the next most frequent interchange, and most originate with adults.

The questions, why and why not, with which children in the popular literature traditionally plague their parents play little part in the repertoire of these children. "Why?" and "why not?" are certainly questions which can be answered by children but are rarely asked. The apparent reason for this disinterest in explanations is evident in the disciplinary processes. Mothers who find their children eating soapsuds out of the washing machine, hanging onto the back of a moving car, or throwing clothespins into the pigpen (all actual examples) do not offer explanations for prohibiting such behavior. Instead, the immediate behavioral consequence is sought without regard to the reasons for compliance. In other words, explanations of "why" are so rarely offered that children do not expect them as a right or source of information.

Therefore, they do not demand to know why. The level of explanation, as in the case of appeals, is non-negotiable. Poverty, age, sex, familial authority, and time-honored socialization techniques are not matters for negotiation, compromise and questioning. Furthermore, the parents do not demand causal explanations from the children. "Why do you throw clothespins at pigs, eat soapsuds or latch onto cars" has all too obvious an answer to mothers. Their children are "bad." The mothers likewise do not proffer an explanation when forbidding such activities to their children. It is the behavior itself and not the motivation, intention, or learning potential of the situation which dictates their actions.

Adults and children ask each other typical questions—who, what, what for, when, where, how. Usually these are requests for information and not for facetious drill. Parents are not in the habit of asking questions to which they already know the answers. Witness the speechlessness and confusion of Fortrel trying to answer his mother's questions, knowing that she already has the answers. (At the direct request of the investigator the mother is attempting to elicit some spontaneous speech from her son.)

NATALIE: What you do in the day?
FORTREL: [*Her four year old son*] Hunh?
NATALIE: What you do in the day? Sit on that chair.
FORTREL: Play.
NATALIE: You play. And what else?
FORTREL: Hunh?
NATALIE: You go sleep?
FORTREL: Hunh?
NATALIE: You go to sleep?
FORTREL: Yeah.

NATALIE: What Scott ate today for dinner?
FORTREL: Hunh?
NATALIE: What Scott ate?
FORTREL: [*Whispers*] Grits.
NATALIE: Well stand up and say it!
FORTREL: Grits.
NATALIE: Grits and what?
FORTREL: And butter.
NATALIE: And what you ate for dinner?
FORTREL: Hunh?
NATALIE: And what you ate for dinner?
FORTREL: Grits?
NATALIE: NO! What did you eat for dinner?
FORTREL: I don't know.
NATALIE: What Warren and them have for dinner today?
FORTREL: Bean.
NATALIE: What kind of bean?
FORTREL: Hunh?
NATALIE: What kind of bean?
FORTREL: Red bean.

Neither do adults indulge in pleasantries: "Did you have a good time playing?" "Did you get enough to eat?" "How do you feel today?" Isn't that a pretty dress?" "What did Santa Claus bring you for Christmas?" There are hundreds of such questions adults might address to children not their own or when talking to their own in front of visitors. In Rosepoint adults do not pretend that children have anything important to say on the above subjects. Special information, yes; polite conversation, no. Paying attention to children's speech is not a canon of politeness.

Only certain kinds of questions will elicit answers from the normally wary, even shy, children of Rosepoint. A question of identity might be answered if phrased "Who you for?" or "Who your mother?" but rarely "What's your name?" "Where is your mama?" rates an answer, but "What are you doing?" "Where have you been?" "What did you do yesterday?" or similar questions dealing with personal activities do not. Questions to which the answer is "yes" or "no" will rate just that and nothing more. Children answer willingly if the questions are phrased to correspond with their experience but do not regard this as a mandate for open-ended answers. Comprehension of the intent and grammatical structure of questions addressed to the child does not mean that he feels any social compulsion to answer.

THE STYLE OF MANIPULATION IN ROSEPOINT

Two styles of language used in the control of children have been contrasted. The style found in Rosepoint is called apodictic. Like the Ten Commandments, it is incontestable and categorical. No mitigating circumstances alter its application. Given certain beliefs about the nature of children and their discipline, the means of control, verbal or not, follow logically. Thus the children are unable to negotiate or bargain about their position vis-à-vis this authority.

An alternative form, illustrated by the personalized family of Bernstein, Haim Ginott's suggested parent-child speech, or the examples from the American middle class, is the practice of "casuistry," the application of general ethical principles to specific cases. The past, the future, and the nature and personality of the individuals involved are taken into consideration. In the process of socialization, language becomes the major element of control. The constant justifications and bargainings become more and more sophisticated.

Casuistry is not the order of life in Rosepoint where there's "no such thing as doesn't and won't."

7/ "Playing around":
the communication of affection
and aggression

INVESTIGATOR: [*To Fortrel*] How old are you?
NATALIE: Tell her how old you is.
FORTREL: Nine?
NATALIE: *No*! Tell her old you is.
FORTREL: Three.
NATALIE: Three, you three.
FORTREL: Three.
INVESTIGATOR: When's your birthday?
FORTREL: Hunh?
LIZ: When's your birthday?
NATALIE: Say December.
FORTREL: December.
NATALIE: The ninth. Say December the ninth.
FORTREL: December ninth.
INVESTIGATOR: How old are you, Anne?
LIZ: How old you are Anne?
ANNE: One.
LIZ: One! [*Everyone laughs.*]
ANNE: Three.
NATALIE: Tell them three.
LIZ: Say I'm three.
ANNE: Three.
FORTREL: Seven.
VISITOR: Fortrel says he's seven.
NATALIE: How old are you?
FORTREL: Seven!

AFFECTION AND AGGRESSION

It takes no Freudian analysis to see that aggression and affection are inextricably intertwined. Shootings and stabbings occurring in Rosepoint within the period of fieldwork averaged two per month. With one exception, they involved the famous "triangle" of stage and screen, a couple and an extra man or woman. If you are implicated in a three-sided relationship, you stand a good chance of being attacked or attacking one of the other members. The rules are very clear and the entire community knows who it is "needs to be shot up a little." Saturday nights and holidays (Christmas, Easter, All Saints' Day, Thanksgiving, New Years) are the likely times. Shooting should be done in private, so as not to involve innocent people. Stabbing, however, is less encompassing and occurs frequently in local bars. The aggrieved party may take vengeance against either spouse or the lover. The community has its rules for determining the guilt, innocence, and proper conduct for these hostilities.

The point of this digression is that there are cultural competences for such performances as aggression. In this case a cultural competence for aggression also includes the competence for affection. One significant manner in which children are trained to this competence can be seen below.

Mothers recall with pride that their children have engaged them in fights and won. With amusement they describe the beatings received at the hands of their husbands. This happens when "I get back at him with my mouth, but sometime my mouth pass too far." Women are allowed verbal aggressions until they are stopped by physical force. Although men rarely resort to verbal violence, women have recourse both to words and blows.

One of the games played with babies, as soon as they are old enough to respond, is a hitting exchange. The mother strikes the infant's hands gently and says, "Don't hit your mama." The baby grins and strikes her back. In very young babies any movement of the hand in response to her action is interpreted as a hit. Everyone laughs and smiles at him when he responds.

For this hitting action the baby receives about as much concentration of approving feedback as he ever receives. Moreover, the game can be divorced from language usage without losing any meaning. Its structure resides in the hit, the merriment, the return blow, and not in any linguistic expectations of adult or child. By nine to twelve months the baby may begin to initiate the exchange. When the child hits the mother or another adult, she says "You gonna hit your mama hunh!" or "You gonna hit me, eh!" Laughter and smiling always follow. No adult is ever threatened by such an act, and the child is positively rewarded.

Sometimes the mother may only smile at the child who shows aggressive behavior toward her. On several occasions a male child challenged her authority and the resulting fight was a pitched battle with none of fighting's niceties. The mothers seemed rather pleased that their boys could beat them up. In these cases witnessed by the investigator the ages ranged from three to eleven. The boys won their immediate point, but the mothers' authority was re-established later. Parents are not threatened or alarmed at all by aggressive physical acts from children, particularly if this is reciprocal. Note the example in Chapter 3 (page 28) in which the boy as calmly threatened to whip his mother as she had threatened him.

Young girls may have an even more subtle range of aggressive-affectionate behavior open to them. The following is illustrative. Three-year-old Anne comes into the living room, adopts a very suggestive, taunting pose, sticks out her index finger, wiggles it, and says:

ANNE: Suck my finger.
MOTHER: [Ignores her.]

ANNE: Suck my finger.
MOTHER: I cut it off.

This is a casual interchange, not angry or threatening. Anne seemed quite satisfied and left to play. The mother treated this as an ordinary event, as later repetitions proved it to be. Occasionally the child would wiggle her finger and suggest the pose by the turn of her head only; the mother responds with a perfunctory, semithreatening gesture in the child's direction. This too seemed to satisfy the requirements of the affectionate exchange. Here again the language which accompanies the full ritual is dispensable. Whatever is communicated, is communicated without it. Ordinarily this exchange retains a certain affectionate quality but occurs between siblings, cousins, and friends. Most of the children do not display these gestures as openly.

The favorite game of children left to their own devices (which is most of the time) is a wrestling game without fighting or talking. Several times the tape recorder was left on in the presence of such activities, in the hope that the children would soon engage in "spontaneous conversation." The resulting tapes, as long as two hours in length, are untranscribable. These auditory records show laughter, and physical movements such as rolling, jumping, running, chasing, and crawling. That which might be transcribed as speech besides laughing includes some proper names, interjections—oh, hey, ow, uh, ha—and various moans, grunts and similar paralinguistic phenomena. If a baby is present, the game is built around him. No objects are employed. The game can be played in the back seat of a car, outside, on the couch, in the street, or any place. It is important to note that the children never fight while playing; the harmony is remarkable. The problem is that the noise level "works on my nerves." The mother becomes irritated and chases them out. Frequently these games are cited as examples of how much children talk! In actuality, as the tapes show, the game is nonlinguistic; it is paralinguistic.

At night when their husbands are home, mothers engage in the same activity with their children. When parents participate, the whole house is an arena; screaming and yelling are allowed. Mothers love this game and sometimes engage in a limited form of it during the day.

A cross-cultural look at training for dependency and aggression is presented in Minturn's and Lambert's *Mothers in six cultures* (1964). The authors present these as a universal set of problems which every child-rearing system must solve.

LOVE GAMES AND LINGUISTIC ROUTINES

Several affectionate games are played by all. Babies are taught how to take part as soon as they learn to talk. The first such game is played between mother and child.

MOTHER: Who you for, chere?
CHILD: You.

MOTHER: [*Laughs*] Who that?
               Who you for, chere?
CHILD: Rosa.
MOTHER: Rosa who?
CHILD: Rosa Abadie   [*Tape*]

The child is supposed to answer with the proper name of his mother. If he says "you," or "mama," she laughs and repeats the game until he answers correctly with her full proper name. Even older children can be surprised into saying "you." No matter what the child answers, the mothers think it funny and laugh. The child is further rewarded by some physical affection, a hug or kiss.

A more popular game allows for gossip and innovation. Any adult and child, or children, can play.

NATALIE: Who KayKay love?
FORTREL: Rat! [*Fortrel is Natalie's three year old son.*]
NATALIE: [*Hearty laugh*] Who!!
FORTREL: Rat!
NATALIE: Oh! That who KayKay love hunh?
               Who I love?
FORTRELS Hunh?
NATALIE: Who I love?
FORTREL: My daddy love you.
NATALIE: [*Hearty laugh*]
LIZ: Who Candy love? [*Liz is Natalie's adult daughter
     and Candy's older sister.*]
FORTREL: Dirk.
LIZ: Dirk.
     And who love Candy?
FORTREL: Dirk.
LIZ: And who love Candy?
FORTREL: Brian.
NATALIE: Brian! [*Everyone thinks this is very funny and laughs appreciatively.*]
                                   [*Tape*]

The real point of this little game is social structure. If the child is sophisticated enough to know the ins and outs of kinship and who is currently sleeping with whom, he will receive substantial rewards for repeating the information. Gossip out of the mouths of babes is strikingly funny. If, however, he is as yet innocent of the ramifications of who loves whom, he will give unsuspecting answers which in their naiveté are just as amusing. Either way he wins.

The child is not being quizzed for the truth value of his statements. The questioners want shocks, the sheer deliciousness of hearing gossip repeated, and amusing new juxtapositions of familiar people. In the above example the child's sister has coaxed him into announcing a triangle. She refuses the reciprocal arrangement between Candy and Dirk that he proposes and makes him pick someone else to love Candy. He obliges and is rewarded by an appreciative round of laughs. Younger children unwittingly couple those for whom love relationships are prohibited on account of incest taboos, the same sex, age differentials, or known animosities. Such possibilities offer endless variety to the game. This game is a testing ground for the child's growing competence in social structure.

EXPRESSIVE COMMUNICATION

The following is from a tape obtained December 18, 1968. The mother, Rosa, has five children of which Mark is the fifth. Mark is at this time twenty-eight months old; his age and the following conversation provide an excellent contrast with Adam and his mother, previously noted in Chapter Five (page 45). Mark's father is a factory worker, and both parents have the equivalent of a junior high education.

ROSA: [*To assembled company of children*] Let them come put the clothes on. Go in the bedroom and change. So they can get out of here. I'm going to get ready. [*to daughter, Cindy*] Come here, Cindy, pick up the broom. Pick up the broom here. [*to Mark*] You want my mama mind you?

MARK: No.   5.

ROSA: You want mama mind you?

MARK: No.

ROSA: You want my mother mind you?

MARK: No.

ROSA: You want your daddy mind you?   10

MARK: No.

ROSA: Who you want to mind you? [*This question and answer dialogue is extremely rapid and fast paced.*]

MARK: No.

ROSA: Want to go ride with me?

MARK: No.   15

ROSA: Hunh?

INVESTIGATOR: He says no to everything.

ROSA: Who this for? [*She is referring to an empty tape reel.*]

MARK: No.

ROSA: Who this for? Romero?   20

MARK: No.

ROSA: [*Louder*] This for Romero?

MARK: [*Louder*] NO.

ROSA: [*Even louder*] Who that for?

MARK: [*Even louder*] NO.   25

ROSA: [*Cajoles*] Who that for, Moogie?

MARK: No.

ROSA: Yeah, that's for Romero.
        These are for Romero.

MARK: No, mine.   30

ROSA: This for *Romero*.

MARK: No, mine.

ROSA: *This* is for Romero.

MARK: No, mine.

ROSA: This *is* for Romero.   35

MARK: No, mine.

ROSA: [*Louder*] This is for Romero!

MARK: No, mine.
ROSA: THIS IS FOR ROMERO!
MARK: NO, MINE!   40
INVESTIGATOR: [*In surprise*] He's saying 'no, mine.'
ROSA: [*To investigator*] Everything he comes in the house he says 'that's mine.'
         Last night I walk in with a big long———— for Rydel. He go 'That's
         mine.'
ROSA: [*To Mark*] This for Romero. [*Firmly enunciated*]   45
MARK: No, mine. [*Just as firmly enunciated*]
ROSA: This for Romero. [*Softly*]
MARK: No, mine. [*Just as softly*]

At this point in the tape she begins to chase him around the living room. They are both laughing; he squeals whenever she comes close. Nothing is said during the chase (timed at two minutes, fifteen seconds by the tape). When she catches him, she kisses and hugs him.

It is impossible to convey on paper the paralinguistic features of this dialogue. The first major section marked by lines 6–17 has the quality of a litany in which participation in the response is more important than the responses themselves. So wrapped up in the rhythm of the exchange are mother and child that they miss inappropriate contributions. The mother asks, "Who you want to mind you?" for which a "no" answer is unsuitable semantically. But the child answers "no" also to an invitation to car riding—the most exciting part of his life—and breaks the smoothness of the chant by intonation as well as content.

The mother's first five questions have a poetic quality about them. This effect is achieved by alternating the membership of one noun class. The paradigm is "you want————to mind you?" The alternating fillers of the class are

$$\left. \begin{array}{l} \text{my mama} \\ \text{mama} \\ \text{my mother} \\ \text{your daddy} \end{array} \right\} = \text{who}$$

The climax to this section, lines 6–15, is a transformation that substitutes the indefinite *who* for the noun class and moves it to the front of the sentence to achieve the optional interrogative form ("Who you want to mind you?"). The other form, of course, is the declarative sentence with interrogative intonation; the first four were of this type.

In line 18 she starts on a new tack, which is unsuccessful. Not only is Mark's vocabulary somewhat limited, but he chooses to answer with "no." The next time she adds the name of his older brother and the resulting "no" is contextually adequate. The variation achieved is not only in noun substitutions within a paradigm, as previously, but in rising intonation patterns as a complement.

The next stanza is lines 18–28. The mother's first three questions (lines 20, 22, 24) are increasingly louder imitating the pattern which characterized the ritual threats. Mark responds in kind to the rising volume. Three is apparently the magic number for maintaining such intensity, so she slows the tempo with a cajoling, flirting question in line 26. The pitch contours of these four questions might be read as [1-3-5-1].[1] The end of the stanza is the self-assured declaration, "yeah, that's for Romero." On his part the child for once does not add to the litany: he knows a good ending when he hears one.

Within this short stanza (lines 20–28) the mother has given him a rich variety of question-answer base rules.

$$\text{who} \quad \left\{ \begin{array}{c} \text{this} \\ \text{that} \end{array} \right\} \quad \text{for} \quad + \quad ? \quad \text{(interrogative intonation)}$$

$$\left\{ \begin{array}{c} \text{this} \\ \text{that} \end{array} \right\} \quad \text{for} \quad \text{Proper Name} \quad + \quad ?$$

It is interesting to note the forms of address used. The child never addresses her at all.[2]

The third stanza (lines 29–36) has a beginning marked by code-switching. The mother switches to the variant *these are* rather than *these* or *this is*. In addition, for her next lines she emphasizes a different word in the sentence each time. Instead of concentrating on syntactic substitutions, transformations, or exocentric intonation patterns, she chooses an endocentric intonation pattern, maintaining the same volume and the same sentence structure but stressing key words in sequence (*these, Romero, this, is*). Mark acknowledges the beginning of this stanza by doubling his output. His "no" contribution becomes "no, mine."

The break between the third stanza and the last (lines 39–48) is relatively minor. Rosa returns to her favorite pattern of rising intonation which is in contrast to the endocentric variation given above. The pitch contours for this stanza read [3-5-3-1]. This stanza is a most satisfying interchange. Every time she raises her pitch (lines 37–44) or changes her tone (lines 45–48), he follows suit. The soft tender ending leads into a more physical expression of their affection and communication.

The mood of the last stanza is fortunately not compromised by the untimely interruption of the anthropologist. Unlike Adam, who donated four hundred of his own utterances in the first taping session (Brown and Fraser 1964), Mark's *mine* was his fourth word in as many months and a landmark occasion. The words were, in order, *Rosa, puppy, no, mine*. Undoubtedly there were others, but the child was difficult to understand. It is evident from this transcript that his need to communicate with his mother and others through words and sentences is minimal. His four words and assorted untranslatable yells are sufficient for his purposes. He was rewarded just as much by this conversation as if he had used more of the pivot structures common in twenty-eight-month-old boys.

It seems likely that this mother is no less compelled to offer him alternative syntactic and intonational groupings than is Adam's mother to expand each structure into her version of a well-formed sentence (Brown and Bellugi 1964:135). To

---

[1] The lowest pitch is 1 and the highest is 5. This is done to account for yelling in ordinary conversation. The noise level in the homes is routinely high enough so that yelling is a necessity. Perhaps it comes to be a habit even in times of relative silence.

[2] She calls him "Moogie," which means *last baby*. When parents decide not to have any more children, they call the final one "Moogie." This is a name which refers to his status in the family, not to his individuality *per se*.

an observer, Mark and his mother's conversation appears boring and pointless, with no clever constructions from him and almost endless, hypnotic repetitiveness from her. Moreover, the subject matter of this discourse is by no means clear.

Contrast this with the obvious concern of Adam and his mother for trucks and their shared experiences of trucks (Brown and Bellugi 1964:135). The differences in what each mother regards as her duty in linguistic socialization are conspicuous. Adam's mother responds to him on the subject of his choosing, paralleling his syntactic constructions and behaving in a nondirective manner. Mark's mother expects a short response, correct or incorrect, but returned *in kind,* matching the mood she has set in the opening. At her instigation, not at his, the conversation begins and the topics change. There is a high level of syntactic predictability. The dialogue is extremely rapid and it is evident from the finale of nonverbal affection-sharing that extraverbal channels of communication are operative.

In short, we have witnessed an episode in the continuing story of how a child acquires a restricted code.

The above dialogue with its high level of structural and lexical predictability meets the requirements for a restricted code.

> If the mother wishes to transmit her discrete experience or her uniqueness, she is unable to do this by varying her verbal selections. She can do it only by varying the messages transmitted through the *extraverbal channels*; through changes in muscular tension if she is holding the child, changes in facial set, gesture, or intonation . . . The mutual intents of mother and child are transmitted through extraverbal channels, and these channels are likely to become objects of special perceptual activity (Bernstein 1964:59).

> An observer might be struck by the fact that the speech in these social relationships was fast, fluent, with reduced articulatory clues, the meanings might be discontinuous, dislocated, condensed and local, but the quantity of speech might not be affected, that there would be a low level of vocabulary and syntactic selection, and that the 'how' rather than the 'what' of the communication would be important (Bernstein 1964:62).

> The status aspect of the social relation is salient (Bernstein 1964:60).

Mark's mother assumes the guiding role. She refers to him here only by his status name as the baby of the family. They do not discuss mutually shared experiences (trucks) but shared statuses[3] (your daddy, my mama) (pages 79–80). Mark has only two lexical items in nineteen utterances; Rosa has eighteen words in twenty utterances; the average sentence length is four words. Other readers may

---

[3] Note that one of Mark's four words is *Rosa,* the name of his mother. He does not use the term mother. While this custom is not the prevailing norm in Rosepoint, it is frequent enough to deserve an explanation. In many of the families older relatives were not addressed by any but personal names, regardless of the kin affiliation to the speaker. One possible hypothesis for this is the interchangeability of family members. All of the seven families studied here had more members than a typical arrangement of father, mother and the children born to them. All of the children have at one time lived for extended periods with their grandmother, great-grandmother, an aunt, or mature sister. Perhaps the flexibility of kin terms reflects the flexibility of the family living groups.

locate new parameters of the restricted code. Bernstein predicts the shape of such a code, particularly the extraverbal channels used for conveying messages. He neglects only the possibility that a restricted code might have lilting, lyrical qualities that are the substance of poetry.

BABY TALK

There are three ways used by parents generally to speak to babies who cannot be counted on to respond in kind. (1) Address him directly as one would any older child who understands. (2) Pretend that one is answering some statement or question he has addressed to you: "Yes, Mama knows you are hungry." (3) Tell him to say something when in fact the statement is directed at some third person: "Tell Daddy you're going to bed now."

Of these three, only the second is not used by the families studied. That form of address involves a pretense surrounding language and the assumption that children can initiate or conduct meaningful conversations with adults. Mothers will attend a baby's needs and wants when he communicates them in the fashion of all babies, but she will not pretend that they are conversing or observe the conventions of conversation. The last alternative, the use of imperatives, is of course a popular one among these mothers.

The grammatical structure of baby talk resembles closely the expansions of the mother's speech to children. She repeats herself continually, alternating syntactic patterns and intonation.

An aunt to her eleven-month nephew:

Hi there big boy,
Hi there Erin,
Hi there big boy.

How you doing big boy?
How you doing Erin?
How you doing big boy?

Unfortunately, more complete information on baby talk is not accessible. From birth to at least six weeks, infants are secluded. This may last until three months, and mothers of infants allow few visitors and rarely take the child out of the house. As a matter of fact, talking to babies is not a common practice. More likely than verbal interaction are kissing, cuddling, playful slaps, rolling on the floor, and other forms of nonverbal interaction.

Mothers do not try to interpret babbling or unclear first words. In other words, they do not impute meaning to sounds which are not yet recognizable words. When asked by the investigator, mothers maintain, "I don't know what she saying." Neither will they repeat what the child has said or attempted to say. Only when the word is recognizable by adult standards is it repeated. Basically, language development at this stage is not overtly encouraged. One mother referred to

Dancing.

her year-old daughter as "good" (rather than the usual "bad"), because she could not yet talk.

In Rosepoint, adults do not expect children to use baby talk as a routine stage in their language development. Descriptions of the reactions of other cultures to using a special language to children (and by extension to animals or lovers) can be found in Casagrande (1948) and Ferguson (1964; 1956).

AFFECTION EXCHANGES

Affection is exchanged nonverbally, as in the case of Mark and his mother, while compliments and verbal encouragements are rare. One little girl constantly begged her mother to buy her something. When it was suggested to the mother that the constant desire for toys, clothes, and food was an appeal for love and reassurance, the mother replied that the child could not understand. Whether it was the words, the concept, or the emotion she could not understand never became clear. However, it is evident that substituting verbal affection for thwarted ownership and poverty was not part of her child-rearing practices. All of the mothers emphasized that children need love, by which they meant the absence of harsh discipline.

Affection and praise are often extended to children, not through language but through the medium of bodily movements and contact. Normally one does not say "thank you," "please," "that's good," "how nice," or similar reinforcements to children. They can be rewarded materially: a nickel, a ride, a hug, toys, candy, or more meat on the beans.

DANCING

Since praise for children is rare, dancing as a rewarded activity deserves mention. Babies who cannot walk will attempt to snap their fingers and move their head in fair imitation of older dancers. Mothers whose children did not shine in tape-recording activities sometimes felt that the children could dance instead. Lavish praise and affectionate encouragement is given to any, children or not, who master the new dance steps or perform the old ones with style. Dancing is the one accomplishment recognized with unstinting praise.

THE REPARATIVE FUNCTION

The term reparative has been suggested by Bernstein:

> We are concerned with the action the mother takes in order that the mother–child relationship can be restored or repaired . . . And to find out how the mother socialises the child into ways by which people discharge their responsibilities to others (Bernstein 1968:22).

Frequently, parents speak harshly to their children, then try to "repair" the damage done the relationship. Theoretically, this repair may be verbal or nonverbal or both, but normal homes provide some way of healing injured feelings. However, what constitutes a threat to the relationship in the first place and what constitutes a bandage for the wound are subject to great variation in cultural definitions. Bernstein asked no questions on this subject, only suggested that it was one mode of language socialization.

In the following paragraphs are three ethnographic examples in which reparations are taking place.

An older sister (twenty-one) hands a piece of banana to her younger brother (five). As he is finishing his portion, he looks at her expectantly. She says very loudly: "NO, YOU NOT GONNA GET NO MORE!" He sits quietly in his chair. A few minutes later she gives him the banana peel with a little bite left in the bottom and tells him in a softer voice: "Go on, go outside and play!"

A two-and-a-half-year old is climbing silently, but actively all over his mother. She appears not to notice, then suddenly screams very loudly: "JOHN!" She pulls him into her lap, hugs him, and they both relax.

A girl, five, asks her mother in a whisper: "You got any money, no?" The mother screams at her very loudly: "YOU AIN'T GETTING ANY!" The child stands there, not a sound. After a pause (perhaps a minute), the mother says quietly: "Catch me my purse."

These examples are typical but are presented as a tentative definition of what speech events constitute the reparative function. Other possibilities could be explored. In the Rosepoint data the offense to the relationship is verbal and very loud. The reconciliation is both verbal and nonverbal: a nickel to spend, a kiss and a hug, or this accompanied by the noticeably softer speech that ends the episode.

In the category of events that do not appear to require a reparative action are name calling, slapping, or the tears of children. Colorful terms for children include "shit-ass," "horse-ass," "ugly bastard," "black bastard," "you-shit," and some which are less common and more impromptu. Strong as these may sound to a middle-class ear for whom "you big baby" is derision, these terms are used publicly, frequently, and occasionally acquire the nature of an affectionate address. Whether a name is accompanied with screaming and a clip to the side of the head or spoken almost softly and jokingly, whether it contains a germ of truth or is insulting, no reparative action is needed.

Affection is often expressed through aggression. Hence, blows may not be damaging to the relationship, but on the contrary, supporting. Taking a swipe at a child whatever the intentions, does not necessitate any immediate compensation, verbal or otherwise. There is no way to evaluate any long-range reparation, that is, delayed by hours or days, because it may go unobserved; if observed, there is no method to tie together the two events in the absence of a more theoretical explanation.

A crying child will not elicit a reparative response, even if he cries in response to some punitive action. "You gonna see what I lay on you," is one conventional reaction of a mother to tears. Another standard reaction to tears is withdrawal— either by an adult or by the child. Sometimes a parent will escape in the car while the child finishes his cry on the doorstep.

Of the activities witnessed which could be termed reparative, none were initiated by children. The child is a passive recipient of reparative action.

EXPRESSIVE FUNCTIONS

The criterion for distinguishing the expressive functions of language is the alteration between verbal and nonverbal means of communication. Only the games of social structure ("Who love me?") and identity ("Who you for?") include no discernible nonverbal segment. They do, however, express affection, and that is perhaps the main emotional component of expressive functions.

The language component, as such, is stereotyped or, as it is called elsewhere, predictable (Bernstein 1964:62). Other factors besides lexical diversification and grammatical complexity convey the messages. The surface structure is deceptively short and simple. Sentences are repeated many times with only minor variations; often only an interrogative, proper name or interjection promote the conversation. The esthetics of the linguistic situation, so to speak, are found in the intonation patterns, rhythm, pitch, stress, and motor activity.

The fallacy that education (that is, socialization) is transmitted primarily by verbal means is refuted. The mode of transmission for a wide range of skills, ideas, and attitudes can be nonverbal or, at most, obliquely verbal.

8 / At home and at school:
observations on discontinuity

The impression must not be left that the children of Rosepoint cannot speak or do not speak well. Nothing is further from the truth. In many instances they choose to remain silent. At play or particularly in the car, they chatter with abandon. Talking as a means of power or control over others is not, however, widely practiced and consequently the children do not learn to control situations verbally. As language development is rewarded only erratically, the children have few cultural incentives to speak up. As a result, the children strike the visitor as extremely pleasant and trustworthy. They can accompany adults anywhere without trouble. There are no "brats" in Rosepoint.

The size of the group to which the child belongs affects his chances for speech expression. In some communities a mother and single child, forced to rely on each other for companionship, may find verbal interaction stimulating. This is not the situation in Rosepoint where the life space is crowded with people. People are the chief resource of the child and the sounds they make are his chief stimuli. Perhaps the constant noise of the television and phonograph offers privacy and security in households whose average density is three per room.

Due to the age-grading system, unqualified love and approval are withdrawn as babies turn into children. This coincides roughly with the age at which the children begin to express themselves verbally. The outcome of the age-grading ideas may be seen in the rapid maturational advances during the first and second year of life when encouragement and acceptance are at their highest. This is followed by a period of slower growth when behavioral expectations (good conduct, quietness, helpfulness) are accelerated. The years from one or two to six, the most crucial for language learning, are the period of least adult contacts and stimulation for these children. In other ways, though, the children mature very rapidly. Their early sense of personal and corporate responsibility is evidence of this.

The Rosepoint child is at his best in peer groups. Here verbal interaction is higher than in family groups which include adults. His experience in interacting with adults has taught him the values of silence or withdrawal. When children are verbal in the presence of adults, it is because other children are nearby to provide the stimulus. Within the peer group, competition is minimized and cooperation maximized. With few toys and many young relatives, a youngster learns from and relies on other children.

The child is not expected gradually to substitute verbal pleasures for nonverbal pleasures. Much of his gratification comes from outside the medium of language. Though the mother yells at him, she also gives him a kind look and a nickel. The requirements are simple and well-defined. While in the house, he has to behave; outside, he has freedom and mobility.

Several sayings summarize local beliefs about children and their learning abilities. "What's in his head ain't in his ass" is a reference to the hardheaded quality of children. Just because they hear a command or know their duties is no guarantee of action. By the same token, this hardheadedness protects them from insult and injury. The belief that parents play little part in language learning is reinforced

An uncle and his niece.

by the lore, "Cut his hair, cut his speech"—if the baby's hair is cut before his first birthday, his language development will be retarded.

THE SCHOOL ENVIRONMENT

The three primary influences on the development of the child are the home, peer groups, and school. As there are no public nursery schools or kindergartens in St. James Parish, and the only private one for blacks is expensive,[1] a child's first exposure to institutionalize education comes after age six. This is late in terms of language learning.

As a result of the integration crisis, the St. James Parish schools are in an unsettled and uncertain state. Though the parish is liberal by Louisiana standards, attempts to retard school integration follow the traditional southern patterns. Recently the parish voted to build two high schools—one for boys and one for girls. The implications of this strategy are obvious. Losing the elementary school in their community (even if it did not have functioning plumbing) is a severe blow to the residents of Rosepoint. Children will be bussed to a new school on the other side of the parish.

Rosepoint parents believe that most of the teachers—black or white—are authoritarian and punitive. Black children attending white schools for the first time are subjected to discriminatory practices, subtle or otherwise. Mothers who complain are treated rudely and the children punished later. One mother complained that the teachers were striking the back of children's hands hard enough to break bones. This, she felt, was wrong. The teacher should hit the palms of the children's hands, a discipline the mother understood from her own school days. The 1960 census reports median school years completed for the non-white population is 4.7. There are, in other words, four times as many people who have never attended a day of high school as have completed high school.[2]

Two aspects of the school situation have direct bearing on family life. One is a lack of communication between class and home. Parents have little notion how the school is run, what their children are taught or how to cooperate in the process. For the most part they worry whether or not the children are observing strict behavioral norms and not about the content of instruction or the child's intellectual progress. From about eleven years old on, staying in school is a touch-and-go proposition, especially for males. On the other hand, the schools show no understanding of the social problems in the parish or the subcultures with which they must cope.

The second feature is the tenuous nature of attendance. The parents will automatically accept any excuse for remaining at home: a tiny blister, no suitable shoes,

---

[1] This private kindergarten costs $15.00 per month for the school year 1968-1969. An increase in this price was scheduled for the school year 1969-1970. With clothes and transportation, this is viewed as too expensive by Rosepoint families.

[2] U.S. Department of Commerce, Bureau of the Census, *United States Census of Population*: 1960, Vol. I, *Characteristics of the Population*, part 20, Louisiana, Table 87, p. 220.

missing the bus (the school is three blocks away), general malaise, or the need for help. Moreover, the teacher may send the child home on the slightest pretext—one effective way of reducing class size. At the first sign of illness or undesirable behavior—imaginary or otherwise—home goes the child. A suspected case of mumps which never materialized rated two weeks at home. Giggling in the halls rated one week. Most missed assignments or temporary irritations are good for the rest of the day. For such judgments there is no court of higher appeal. The child remains home the alloted time. Attendence patterns are significant since in some families a school day rarely passes (and for some families, never passes) in which only the preschoolers are home. On any given day a sampling of older children will be present. Some nuclei of siblings are rarely separated from each other.

THE CONFLICT OF HOME AND SCHOOL

If the *cultures* of home and school are in conflict, which captures the mind of a child? The irrelevancy of the school for most Rosepoint children is measured by the high dropout rate, the low rates of literacy, and an abiding urban and rural poverty in Louisiana.

The school creates for the Rosepoint child an environment not as much unpleasant as unnatural. For years he has been determining his own schedule for eating, sleeping, and playing. The content of his play is unsupervised and depends on the child's imagination. His yard does not contain sand boxes, swings, clay, paints, nor personnel obliged to supervise his play. At school, however, play is supervised, scheduled, and centers around objects deemed suitable for young minds. There are firm schedules for playing, napping, eating, and "learning and studying," (with the implication that learning will occur only during the time alloted for it). The authority buttressing even minimal schedules is impersonal and inflexible with an origin not in face-to-face social relationships but in an invisible bureaucracy.

Moreover, the Rosepoint home relies on verbal communication rather than on the written word as a medium. Adults do not read to children nor encourage writing. Extraverbal communication such as body movements or verbal communication such as storytelling or gossip are preferred to the printed page. The lack of money to purchase books, magazines, and newspapers partly explains this. However, access to public libraries, bookmobiles, and cheap pulp publications is seldom utilized. Perhaps the schools are at fault in not encouraging better reading habits. Yet, for children of a culture rich in in-group lore and oral traditions the written word is a pallid substitute. Whatever the reason, a child unconvinced of the need to commit his thoughts to paper is primed for trouble at school.

Another conflict arising out of the home–school discrepancy is language—specifically, "bad" language. Remember that the Rosepoint child is rewarded for linguistic creativity. At a family gathering, one two-year old girl just learning to talk said to her mother and her aunt: "Fuck you, you cow!" She was greeted with hearty laughter, a kiss, and approval. Later that month, the child's mother and aunt in speaking to a close mutual friend recounted the story with relish. They were careful, of course, to whom they related the episode, knowing that some would be shocked at this manner of addressing one's elders. But the child's growing mastery of language was not construed as a threat or insult.

In the classroom such language has an entirely different interpretation placed on it. Some educators discretely refer to it as "the M-F problem."[3] (The problem originates with the educators and not the child.) A nine-year-old girl was given a two-week suspension from classes for saying a four-letter word. This was her first recorded transgression of the language barrier. The second offense may be punished by expulsion. In such cases, the child's low grades are not a reflection of performance or intelligence, but the result of enforced absences. Children get kicked out of school for verbal infractions whether teachers and administrators are black or white. This puts the M-F problem more on the level of class than color.

That these children are not placed in competitive roles in their preschool days is a point to be emphasized. Overt peer and sibling rivalries are noticeably absent. In Rosepoint a child is exposed far more often to the values and portrayal of genuine cooperation. For another example of a society cherishing cooperation more than competition see Margaret Mead's *Coming of Age in Samoa* (1967). In the classroom, "cooperating," instead of competing, may be called cheating on a test, not trying hard enough, or not working up to potential.

The future as an idea and the preparations necessary for it motivate many of the school's policies. Getting into college, getting a job, or getting good grades are rationalizations for a given event years in advance of the event. Punishment is sometimes deferred far beyond the time span of the guilty action, cards reporting "citizenship grades" being a case in point. The moral force of the middle-class principle of delayed gratification—work now, get paid later—is inappropriate for people who have not found the pot of gold at the end of the hard work.

In the types of testing situations which determine grades or measure achievement and I.Q., the Rosepoint child is at a disadvantage. He has not received the constant drill which is characteristic of the middle-class mother and child interaction. Nor has he been trained in a specialized set of verbal skills called "correct grammar" the mastery of which is a measure of pedagogical success. He may have only limited access to that bank of childhood minutiae somehow crucial to classroom achievement.

Some as yet unanswered questions suggested by the discord between home and school cultures are:

(1) If the teachers in public schools talk like Adam's mother (in Chapter 5) rather than like Kenneth's or Mark's mother, what happens to the processes of communication?

(2) Can students learn the "language" of the teacher if the teacher does not know their "language?"

(3) What happens to students raised in a positionalized home confronted with teachers who operate on a personalized basis?

---

[3] Refers to the use of obscenities in school, including "motherfucker."

DUMB OR DEPRIVED?

It would probably not be difficult to predict the scores of these children on intelligence examinations. Which of these tests uses familiar words like "bayou," "bisque," "lagniappe," "parrain," "crayfish," "creole," or "levee"? Nor do expressions such as "making a birthday," "having a baby for Clement," "pass to the road," or "bring me ride" occur on standard achievement tests. Queries regarding directions, "north," "south," "east," or "west," may confuse a child who thinks in terms of "up the river," "down the river," "away from the river," and "to the river." Rosepoint children know the intricacies of the sugar-cane cycle but have never experienced snow. Are children who identify carrots as sweet potatoes dumb? Add to this the fact that for these children the test-taking situation is alien, the goals for such activity obscure, and the cultural expectations for performance minimal.

The notion that low scores on intelligence tests or bad grades in school indicate "cultural deprivation" is false. Individuals required to take an exam in a culture and dialect not their own will necessarily appear stupid. Tests to measure competency in the *culture* of the rural, black, and poor have not yet been invented.

THE VALUES OF THE ROSEPOINT WAY

These techniques of language socialization stem in part from the family system. In nuclear families those who have no authority over the children likewise have no responsibility and the child is left in a precarious position when one or both of his parents are absent. The strength and flexibility of the Rosepoint family lie, however, in interchangeability. If the children have a neurotic mother, an absent father, or a handicapped sibling, the family is not maimed. Its completeness is insured through the extended family. Adults who can offer maternal and paternal love are ready to assume these responsibilities. Assistance comes in the form of money, in adopting and raising each other's children, and, above all, in furnishing the emotional support often lacking in nuclear families forced on their own resources. This, for the children, is a healthy situation. The range of those people who can spank or discipline the children is increased, but then so is the range of those who will give a nickel, a car ride, some food, security, and succor.

Child-rearing techniques stem from a sense of tradition and a shared belief about the proper way to raise children. This consistency is found less frequently in middle-class families who raise their children "by the book" or follow various developmental schemes. Ideas of the proper discipline are not, for example, fully shared even by members of the immediate family. Thus for Rosepoint the level of ambiguity is reduced both for the children who are exposed to the one prevailing method and for the mothers whose confidence and authority are buttressed by each other. No family or child is wholly dependent on the whims of one member.

The language component of child-rearing techniques likewise reduces ambiguity by its clarity and consistency. If a mother expects her child to be quiet, she says "Be quiet" or words to that effect. Such a behavioral expectation is not considered novel or difficult for him to execute. Her tactics are straightforward. Tricking him by teasing, sarcasm, or indirect allusions is alien to her style. In the child's own home or at another's, the mother's approaches to obtaining quiet will be the same. The advantage from the child's viewpoint is the security which comes from a unified tradition of child-rearing.

An important concomitant of the linguistic socialization process is the sameness of social expectations. Unlike mobile middle-class families, Rosepoint children are not expected to enhance their parents' reputations. A mother is not known by the children she keeps. The children are free of the pressure to show off to please parents. They are expected to mind, to cooperate, and to grow up, not to be miniature Shirley Temples. If a child's speech is hesitant, his clothes dirty or torn, his manners rudimentary or behavior silly, so what—this is the natural condition of childhood. In Rosepoint everyone knows and accepts the fact that children are just like that.

Additional readings

BERNSTEIN, BASIL, 1961, Social structure, language, and learning. *Educational Research* 3: 163–178. Also in J. De Cecco (ed.), *The Psychology of Language, Thought, and Instruction: Readings*, New York: Holt, Rinehart and Winston, Inc., pp. 89–103.

————, 1964, Elaborated and restricted codes: their social origins and some consequences. In J. J. Gumperz and D. Hymes (eds.), *The Ethnography of Communication*, American Anthropologist Special Publication 66 (2), pp. 55–69.

————, 1965, A sociolinguistic approach to social learning. In J. Gould (ed.), *Penquin Survey of the Social Sciences*, Baltimore: Penquin Books, pp. 144–168.

In the above articles, Bernstein makes a major point. Differences in the use of language in working class and middle-class child-rearing practices result in two "codes" or two language styles in English. A communication gap is created because children bring to the schools perceptions based on conflicting linguistic codes.

FRAZIER, E. FRANKLIN, 1966, *The Negro Family in the United States*. Revised and abridged edition with a new foreword by Nathan Glazer. Chicago: University of Chicago Press.

An analysis of the history and sociological factors behind the black family in America which shows the family structure as a product of the massive social and economic changes which swept up first the slave and later the free man.

LENNEBERG, ERIC H. (ed.), 1966, *New Directions in the Study of Language*. Cambridge, Massachusetts: The M.I.T. Press.

The interdisciplinary articles by Carmichael, Miller, Lenneberg, Brown and Bellugi, and Ervin present controversial linguistic theories with their implications for verbal behavior.

ROHRER, JOHN H., AND MUNRO S. EDMONSON (eds.), 1960, *The Eighth Generation Grows Up: Cultures and Personalities of New Orleans Negroes*. New York: Harper and Row, Publishers.

This fascinating study of black families in New Orleans is a follow-up of the classic book *Children of Bondage* (Allison David and John Dollard, eds.). The social structure and minority group experiences of these urban black children parallel in many ways those of the nearby rural children.

SLOBIN, DAN I. (ed.) *et al.,* 1967, *A Field Manual for Cross-Cultural Study of the Acquisition of Communicative Competence*. Berkeley: University of California Press.

Useful suggestions for investigating how children learn language. In addition to some tips on research methodology, it contains bibliographies and theoretical summaries.

WHITING, BEATRICE B. (ed.), 1963, *Six Cultures: Studies of Child-Rearing*. New York: John Wiley and Sons, Inc.

These readable ethnographic studies of socialization in communities in India, Africa, Mexico, Okinawa, the Philippines, and New England are excellent sources for cross-cultural comparison. Printed in separate paperback editions, the first volume, *Field Guide for a Study of Socialization*, John M. Whiting, *et al.* (eds.), is very helpful on methodology for studying children and family structure.

Volume Five, *The New Englanders of Orchard Town, U.S.A.*, by John and Ann Fischer, investigates child-rearing practices in white middle-class families which could be used as a basis for comparison with Rosepoint.

A follow-up volume called *Mothers in Six Cultures*, by Leigh Minturn and William B. Lambert (John Wiley and Sons, 1964) compares specific techniques and attitudes of mothers and caretakers in these six cultures.

WHITTEN, NORMAN E., AND J. F. SZWED (eds.), 1970, *Afro-American Anthropology: Contemporary Perspectives on Theory and Research.* Foreword by Sidney Mintz. New York: The Free Press.

This collection of readings on the black man in the New World provides a much-needed cross-cultural perspective. In particular, the articles on family structure in America and around the Caribbean show a vital, adapting family life which is more than a passive reaction to socioeconomic conditions. The few articles on language provide an alternative to the idea of dialect as linguistic deprivation.

References cited

ANASTASI, A., AND C. DE JESÚS, 1953, Language development and nonverbal I.Q. of Puerto Rican preschool children in New York City. *Journal of Abnormal Social Psychology* 48: 357–66.

BARKER, ROGER G., AND HERBERT WRIGHT, 1954, *Midwest and Its Children*. Evanston, Illinois: Row, Peterson and Co.

BELLUGI, URSULA, 1965, The development of interrogative structures in children's speech. In K. F. Riegel (ed.), *The Development of Language Functions*, Ann Arbor, Mich.: University of Michigan Center for Human Growth and Development 8, pp. 103–37.

BERKO, JEAN, 1958, The child's learning of English morphology. *Word* 14: 150–77. Also in S. Saporta (ed.), 1961, *Psycholinguistics: A Book of Readings*, New York: Holt, Rinehart and Winston, Inc., pp. 359–75.

BENEDICT, RUTH, 1946, *Chrysanthemum and the Sword*. Boston: Houghton Mifflin Company.

BERNSTEIN, BASIL, 1962, Social class, linguistic codes and grammatical elements. *Language and Speech* 5:221–40.

———, 1964, Elaborated and restricted codes: their origins and some consequences. In J. J. Gumperz and D. Hymes (eds.), *The Ethnography of Communication*, American Anthropologist Special Publication 66 (6), pp. 55–69.

———, 1968, A sociolinguistic approach to socialization with some references to educability. Unpublished manuscript. Sociological Research Unit, University of London Institute of Education.

———, 1968, A coding grid for analysing questions on social control between mothers and their children. Unpublished manuscript. Sociological Research Unit, University of London Institute of Education.

BERNSTEIN, BASIL, AND DOUGLAS YOUNG, 1968, Social class differences in conceptions of the use of toys. *Sociology* 1:131–40.

BOURGEOIS, LILLIAN C., 1957, *Cabanocey: The History, Customs and Folklore of St. James Parish*. New Orleans: Pelican Press.

BRAINE, MARTIN D. S., 1963, The ontogeny of English phrase structure: the first phrase. *Language* 39:1–13.

BROWN, ROGER, AND URSULA BELLUGI, 1964, Three processes in the child's acquisition of syntax. In E. H. Lenneberg (ed.), *New Directions in the Study of Language*, Cambridge, Mass.: The M.I.T. Press, pp. 131–62.

BROWN, ROGER, AND COLIN FRASER, 1963, The acquisition of syntax. In C. N. Cofer and B. S. Musgrave (eds.), *Verbal Behavior and Learning: Problems and Processes*, New York: McGraw-Hill Book Company, pp. 159–97.

CASAGRANDE, JOSEPH B., 1948, Comanche baby talk. *International Journal of American Linguistics* 14:11–14.

CAZDEN, C. B., 1965, Environmental assistance to the child's acquisition of grammar. Unpublished doctoral dissertation, Harvard University.

CHASE, RICHARD ALLEN, 1966, Evolutionary aspects of language development and function. In T. Smith and G. Miller (eds.), *The Genesis of Language: A Psycholinguistic Approach*, Cambridge, Mass.: The M.I.T. Press, pp. 253–68.

COULON, KERMIT, 1965, *St. James Parish History and Resources*. Louisiana Cooperative Extension Service; St. James Parish, Convent, Louisiana.

DUFOUR, CHARLES, 1967, *Ten Flags in the Wind: The Story of Louisiana*. New York: Harper and Row, Publishers.

ERVIN, SUSAN M., 1966, Imitation and structural change in children's language. In E. H. Lenneberg (ed.), *New Directions in the Study of Language*, Cambridge, Mass.: The M.I.T. Press, pp. 163–89.

EVANS-PRITCHARD, E. E., 1967, *The Nuer: A Description of the Modes of Livelihood and Political Institutions of a Nilotic People*. Oxford: Clarendon Press.

FISCHER, J. L., 1964, Words for self and others in some Japanese families. In J. J. Gumperz and D. Hymes (eds.), *The Ethnography of Communication*, American Anthropologist Special Publication 66 (2), pp. 115–26.

FISCHER, JOHN L. AND ANN, 1966, *The New Englanders of Orchard Town, U.S.A. Six Culture Series*, vol. 5. New York: John Wiley and Sons, Inc.

FORTIER, ALCÉE, 1895, *Louisiana Folk Tales*. Boston: Houghton Mifflin Company.

———, 1904, *History of Louisiana*. 4 vols. New York.

FERGUSON, CHARLES A., 1964, Baby talk in six languages. In J. J. Gumperz and D. Hymes (eds.), *The Ethnography of Communication*, American Anthropologist Special Publication 66 (2), pp. 103–14.

GINOTT, HAIM, 1965, *Between Parent and Child: New Solutions to Old Problems*. New York: The Macmillan Company.

GUMPERZ, JOHN J., 1964, Linguistic and social interaction in two communities. In J. J. Gumperz and D. Hymes (eds.), *The Ethnography of Communication*, American Anthropologist Special Publication 66 (2), pp. 137–53.

HYMES, DELL, 1961, Functions of speech: an evolutionary approach. In F. Gruber (ed.), *Anthropology and Education*, Philadelphia: University of Pennsylvania Press, pp. 55–83.

———, 1962, The ethnography of speaking. In T. Gladwin and W. C. Sturtevant (eds.), *Anthropology and Human Behavior,* Washington, D.C.: Anthrop. Soc. Wash., pp. 13–53.

———, 1964, Introduction: toward ethnographies of communication. In J. J. Gumperz and D. Hymes (eds.), *The Ethnography of Communication*, American Anthropologist Special Publication 66 (2), pp. 1–29.

LENNEBERG, ERIC (ed.), 1966, *New Directions in the Study of Language*. Cambridge, Mass.: The M.I.T. Press.

———, 1967, *Biological Foundations of Language*. New York: John Wiley and Sons, Inc.

LYON, J., AND R. J. WALES, 1966, *Psycholinguistics Papers*. The proceedings of the 1966 Edinburgh Conference. Edinburg University Press.

MCNEILL, DAVID, 1966, Developmental psycholinguistics. In T. Smith and G. Miller (eds.), *The Genesis of Language: A Psycholinguistics Approach*, Cambridge, Mass.: The M.I.T. Press, pp. 15–84.

MEAD, MARGARET, 1967, *Coming of Age in Samoa*. New York: Dell Publishing Co., Inc.

MENYUK, P., 1964, Syntactic rules used by children from preschool through first grade. Child Development Monograph 35:533–46.

MILLER, WICK, AND SUSAN M. ERVIN, 1964, The development of grammar in child language. In U. Bellugi and R. Brown (eds.), *The Acquisition of Language*, Child Development Monograph 29:9–34.

MINTURN, LEIGH, AND WILLIAM LAMBERT, 1964, *Mothers in six cultures*. New York: John Wiley and Sons, Inc.

ROBINSON, W. P., n.d., Social factors and language development in primary school children. Unpublished manuscript. Sociological Research Unit, Institute of Education, University of London.

SACHS, HARVEY, AND H. GARFINKEL (eds.), 1969, *Contributions in Ethnomethodology*. Bloomington, Ind.: Indiana University Press.

SCHATZMANN, LEONARD, AND ANSELM STRAUSS, 1966, Social class and modes of communication. In Alfred G. Smith (ed.), *Communication and Culture*, New York: Holt, Rinehart and Winston, Inc., pp. 442–55.

SLOBIN, DAN I. (ed.) *et al.*, 1967, *A Field Manual for Cross-Cultural Study of the Acquisition of Communicative Competence*. Berkeley: University of California Press.

———, 1968, Questions of language development in cross-cultural perspective. Manuscript prepared for Symposium "Language learning in cross-cultural perspective," Michigan State University, East Lansing; Sept. 25, 1968.

SNELL, DAVID, 1969, Dateline America: a waning echo in Cajun country. *Life* 66–10:188.

U.S. DEPARTMENT OF COMMERCE. Bureau of the Census. *United States Census of Population: 1960*. Vol. 1 *Characteristics of the Population*, pt. 20, Louisiana.

WEIR, RUTH, 1962, *Language in the Crib*. The Hague: Mouton.